Swedish Cinema, from Ingeborg Holm to Fanny and Alexander

By PETER COWIE

THE SWEDISH INSTITUTE

Peter Cowie was born in England in 1939, and has specialised in Swedish cinema since the late 1950's, when he first became aware of the work of Ingmar Bergman. Educated at the University of Cambridge, he is the Editor *International Film Guide* and author of more than a dozen books, including a recent critical biography of Bergman. Peter Cowie served as the only non-Nordic member of the Swedish Film Institute's Quality Awards Jury for eleven years.

The author alone is responsible for the opinions expressed in this book.

This book is for Anna-Maija.

Design and cover: Vidar Forsberg

100 17 89857

Printed in Sweden by Stellan Ståls Tryckerier AB, Stockholm 1985
ISBN 91-520-0162-8

CONTENTS

Silence is Golden, 1909—1924   5
The emergence of Swedish film companies   5
Victor Sjöström   8
Mauritz Stiller   15

Surviving the Thirties and Forties: The Quest for Commitment   23
Cinema as diversion   23
Gustaf Molander   25
Back to earth—socio-political themes start to emerge   27
Newcomers to the Forties scene   30
Hasse Ekman   32
Alf Sjöberg   32

The Rise of Ingmar Bergman   37
Bergman's apprentice years   37
Two masters emerge   43
 Ingmar Bergman   46
 Alf Sjöberg   49
Bergman achieves world status   50
Other gifted directors   59
 Arne Mattsson   61
 Arne Sucksdorff   62

A New Era, 1962—1970   64
The creation of the Film Institute   64
Pioneers of the Sixties   67
Freedom of expression: love and sex in the Sixties   68
 Bo Widerberg   69
 Jörn Donner   73

Vilgot Sjöman	73
Mai Zetterling	77
The porn syndrome	79
One man's fate	80
Bergman's response to the spirit of the Sixties	84
Social and political films	89
The documentary factor	93
Two new talents emerge	99
Jonas Cornell	100
Kjell Grede	102
The Most Recent Wave	105
Modern Swedish society in films	105
Glancing back	111
Comedy	115
Offbeat approaches	120
Modern literature on screen	125
Thrillers	127
The return of Jan Troell	129
Films for children	130
Bergman: The latest phase	135
Today—and tomorrow?	143

9152001628

Silence is Golden, 1909–1924

There is no more stirring feat in the entire history of silent film than the Swedish achievements between 1913 and 1921. The Swedes allowed the Americans a head-start of at least ten years, but once Victor Sjöström and Mauritz Stiller hit their stride, the world looked to Stockholm for craftsmanship and imagination in cinema.

The beginnings were cautious and somewhat ponderous, like many a Scandinavian response to new artistic movements. In February, 1895, the Edison "Kinetoscope" was unveiled to audiences in Stockholm (and Rune Waldekranz has reminded us that the German film pioneer Ottomar Anschütz sent his famous "Schnellseher" to the first photographic exhibition at the Stockholm Palace of Industry in November of the previous year). But the public at large did not become aware of the cinema as a spectacle for some years. The Court photographer, Ernest Florman, made some farces, but they only furthered the notion that this visual novelty was but an extension of the circus—a harmless spectacle far removed from the realms of art.

The emergence of Swedish film companies

Two men set Swedish cinema on its auspicious course. Charles Magnusson had, as a young man of 19, attended the first exhibitions of Lumière films in Malmö in 1896, and resolved to become a cameraman. By 1905 he was starting to make a name as a newsreel photographer of great integrity and courage. He shot the state entry of King Haakon of Norway into Kristiania on November 25, 1905, and despite thick fog produced a report superior to any filmed by those foreign cameramen present at the occasion.

In 1909, Charles Magnusson joined a youthful company known as "Svenska Bio" in Kristianstad (in southern Sweden). Launched by two enterprising businessmen, Wiberg and Nylander, Svenska Bio would, in 1919, be incorporated into the world-famous name of "Svensk Filmindustri" (SF). From the start, Svenska Bio bolstered its activity by acquiring up to 20 movie theatres, thus providing a ready outlet for its own productions, a tradition that continues to this day in Sweden. Although Kristianstad was then the main centre of film activity in the country, the work of Erik Dahlberg in Stockholm should not be overlooked. Dahlberg specialised in historical dramas on screen.

In 1910, Julius Jaenzon came to work at Svenska Bio. There are really four outstanding figures in the Swedish silent cinema: Victor Sjöström, Mauritz Stiller, Charles Magnusson—and Julius Jaenzon, whose superb camerawork set a benchmark for every other cinematographer in Europe, who shot virtually all the great masterpieces of Sjöström and Stiller, and then passed on his secrets to a new generation, including Ingmar Bergman's colleague, Gunnar Fischer, in the 1930's and 1940's.

It is a fallacy that Sjöström and Stiller were the first regular filmmakers working under Magnusson. In the autumn of 1909, for example, the actor Carl Engdahl, engaged by Magnusson as a director, completed *The People of Värmland* ("Värmlänningarna"), together with two cameramen, Robert Ohlson and Ernst Dittmar. Here one finds the first evidence of the bucolic, folkloric tinge that was to colour so much of Swedish cinema in the years ahead.

Magnusson's pronouncements reveal him as a producer of rare vision and good sense. He realised that the public must be absorbed in what was happening on the screen: "The action is the motion picture's Alpha and Omega. It should ... give opportunities for intensely exciting and interesting situations." On the freedom granted to his directors: "The film producer must be supreme ruler. He alone decides ... but after he has given the starting signal, he should leave the director in peace. If the director is unworthy of this confidence, he is not fit to be a director."

In other countries, the primitive cinema was intent on reproducing the virtues of the theatre. Staging was all. Magnusson, however, felt

Julius Jaenzon.

that both the visuals and the performances on screen should be free of the limitations of stage productions. By 1911 he had expanded his production range to include a series of travel films, shot mainly by Julius Jaenzon, and later that year Svenska Bio moved to Stockholm, where a studio was built in the suburb of Lidingö. By the spring of the following year, the buildings were ready, and Magnusson began looking for good directors. The first man he contacted was Georg af Klercker, who had been born in Kristianstad and had served as a lieutenant with the aristocratic Svea Life Guards in Stockholm.

Klercker was head of the Lidingö studios until he broke off on his own and joined the Hasselblad studios in Gothenburg. None of his films from the Svenska Bio days are extant, but when one inspects the few films of Klercker's that have survived—all from the Gothenburg years—one is forced to recognise that here was a major talent, a man who, had he somehow been able to work in conjunction with Stiller and Sjöström, might have enjoyed as great a renown as they did.

Several of the 27 features Klercker completed at Hasselblad were enhanced by the ethereal beauty of Mary Johnson, an actress who would reach her apogee as Elsalill in Stiller's *Sir Arne's Treasure*. Mood and composition, however, distinguish Klercker's work more than performances. In *The Victory of Love* ("Kärleken segrar", 1916), he anticipates the deep-focus photography deployed by Renoir during the 1930's. Using a system of lenses perfected by Hasselblad, Klercker seems equally at ease with natural or artificial light. In *The Mystery of the Night of the 24th* ("Mysteriet natten till den 25:e", 1916), the atmosphere is strongly reminiscent of Louis Feuillade's tongue-in-cheek thrillers. This is a three-act "sensational drama" featuring Cony Hoops, the celebrated detective. A murderer at a party is caught by Hoops and vows revenge on him. The Black Band gang swiftly enter the picture, trapping Hoops in a dark cottage, and placing a time bomb beside him as he sits bound to a chair. The cottage is blown to smithereens but of course Hoops pops up unscathed, and is soon embroiled again with the Band at Valincourt Castle. As one fantastic and mesmerising episode succeeds another, Klercker's ingenuity yields constant surprises. There are the fluorescent shots of a torch pointed into the camera as a villain advances down a narrow stairway, and the cunning visual deceptions of the "secret mirror door" in the castle.

Victor Sjöström

Victor Sjöström had become loved and respected as an actor on the travelling theatre circuit in both Sweden and Finland. In February, 1912, he was rehearsing *A Midsummer Night's Dream* in Malmö, and was startled by a telephone call one evening from Erik Ljungberger, an old friend and neophyte screenwriter, who had raised Sjöström's name in conversation with Charles Magnusson. Svenska Bio were offering Sjöström a contract, with a lot of money attached. From May 1, 1912, he began his career as a film-maker although he had already been intrigued by an earlier visit to Paris with Magnusson to observe work at the Pathé studio.

"The thing that brought me to film-making," declared Sjöström, "was a youthful desire for adventure and a curiosity to try this new medium of which I then did not have the slightest knowledge." At first he had to fit in with Svenska Bio's hectic production schedule, churning out farces and historical epics to satisfy the daily demand at the box-office. He appeared as an actor in several of his own and Stiller's films, and immediately demonstrated his gifts as a film-maker on his debut behind the cameras with – *The Gardener,* also known as *The Broken Spring Rose* ("Trädgårdsmästaren", 1912) with its numerous location scenes and the audacious playing of Lili Beck (soon to become the second Mrs. Sjöström).

The cinema was still not recognised as an art. "Decent people wanted nothing to do with it," Sjöström said, "and I remember that we were most ashamed when we were forced to go out on location in streets and public places." Still, Sjöström was sufficiently enthused by his first season at Lidingö that he decided to devote most of his career to films, even if he still cherished the theatre. *Ingeborg Holm* (1913), sometimes called *Give Us This Day,* was his first authentic masterpiece, and may be defended as the most thoughtful and controlled of all films prior to *Birth of a Nation* made in the United States in 1915. Based on a stage play about a woman who falls foul of the public welfare authorities in Helsingborg, *Ingeborg Holm* created a furious controversy in the press. The cruelty of a widow's having her child snatched from her side by the welfare authorities, resulting in the woman's own descent into madness, placed the Poor Law Commission in an extremely bad light. On October 27, 1913, a reviewer in Gothenburg wrote: "We have seen good films made by Swedish artists, but none that can compete with this." Newspapers in Denmark and England were soon echoing this

A scene from *Ingeborg Holm* (1913).

acclaim. The film has a tension and a conviction that are unusual for the period, and demonstrate a readiness on Sjöström's part to take his camera out of doors and to achieve authenticity in even the tiniest details.

In 1916, Sjöström took some leave, and made a sentimental journey to the places where he had lived as a child, in the lush pastoral landscape of Värmland. His cycle tour took him on to Norway, and to Grimstad, where Henrik Ibsen had first heard the story of Terje Vigen, the sailor who ran foul of the English blockade of Norway during the Napoleonic Wars. Svenska Bio had been hoping to film the poem for some time; Sjöström had been sceptical, but now he saw the essence of Terje Vigen's personality. From this point on, his attitude became that of the pantheist. God is present in nature, as are goodness and evil, and all the influences in a man's life. A cable to Magnusson was the signal for preparations on the movie to begin. In *Terje Vigen* (1916), for the first time in the cinema, the landscape reflects the struggles between the characters and within themselves. Two French film historians described the film as "an intimate *Song of Roland,* celebrating the sea and the men who live with it, denouncing the wickedness of war and the ambitions of dictatures, and pitying the lot of the man whom war has removed from all he holds dear and who finds himself alone." The film is swept along by Sjöström's feeling for setting and atmosphere, by the almost prehensile attacks of the sea, and by the brilliantly syncopated editing, which is at its most impressive in the scene where Terje rows desperately away from an English frigate's boat. Sjöström alternates close-ups of Terje's weary arms heaving the oars back and forth with shots of the well-drilled English crew slipping easily through the breakers. The sea is Terje's real foe, and there is a magnificent back view of Terje (played by Sjöström) shaking his fists at the boiling waves.

Shooting on *Terje Vigen* took almost three months, and the production cost three times as much as the normal Svenska Bio release. The gamble was a huge one, but it proved successful, with 53 prints being sold abroad—and the reviews were ecstatic. In a cinema in Denmark, one woman was so overcome that she began reciting Ibsen's poem loudly in the darkness. And although the film did not reach the United States until 1920 (under the title, *A Man There Was*), the response was equally warm. "Victor Seastrom should come to America and teach his competitors how to make films," wrote one reviewer.

Sjöström now began to devote more time to each project, and in this he had the far-sighted support of his boss, Charles Magnusson. However, the spring and summer of 1917 were more than busy. Sjöström shot *The Girl from the Marsh Croft* ("Tösen från Stormyrtorpet") and *The Outlaw and His Wife* ("Berg-Ejvind och hans hustru") back to back. The films could not have been more different to each other. *The*

Splendid use of mountain scenery in *The Outlaw and His Wife*.

Girl from the Marsh Croft is in the same idiom as *Ingeborg Holm*—with a girl made pregnant by a well-to-do farmer, and a sense of outrage at the exploitation of the underprivileged. *The Outlaw and His Wife*, however, pursues the line of *Terje Vigen*, championing the individual's struggle against a hostile society and a relentless foe—Nature. As the Icelandic outlaw forced to climb ever higher into the mountains to evade capture by the sheriff, Berg-Ejvind is a forerunner of the Knight in Bergman's *The Seventh Seal*, refusing to give in to the inevitable, and joining his dead wife in a snow-covered grave. He survives to this point

Sjöström both directed and played the role of David Holm in *Thy Soul Shall Bear Witness*.

by virtue of his physical courage, illustrated in a vivid sequence when he dangles on a rope over a high cliff and is only hauled to safety just in time (during filming, Sjöström nearly lost his life when this stunt went awry).

Prominent too in this masterpiece is the Scandinavian approach to the seasons. Summer is recalled in short, wrenching spasms, as the outlaw sits starving in his mountain hut towards the end; but winter, equated in the Swedish arts with death, destroys the spirit and whips the snow over the couple's bodies with inexorable force.

The popular novelist, Selma Lagerlöf (1858–1940), whose books portrayed Sjöström's native province of Värmland, became a fruitful source for Swedish films during this era. As Carl Dreyer once commented, "Selma Lagerlöf's predilection for dreams and supernatural events appealed to Sjöström's own somewhat sombre artistic mind." The two-part film made by Sjöström from *The Sons of Ingmar* ("Ingmarssönerna", 1918) was seen by 196,000 people in Stockholm alone, and its immense commercial success enabled Magnusson to take over his rivals and form Svensk Filmindustri, as well as to erect new studios at Råsunda. The sequel, *Karin, Daughter of Ingmar* ("Karin Ingmarsdotter", 1920), again involved Sjöström in hazardous stunt work (plunging waist-deep into an icy river, for example), and even today remains a fluent film. "Indeed, its formal, plastic qualities," wrote the English critic, John Gillett, in 1978, "and the ease with which Sjöström breaks up his sequences into very modern-looking close, medium and long shots, make it difficult to believe that the film was made nearly sixty years ago."

The crowning glory of Sjöström's work in Sweden was *Thy Soul Shall Bear Witness,* also known as *The Phantom Carriage* ("Körkarlen", 1921) which was taken from a novel by Selma Lagerlöf and offered Julius Jaenzon the most taxing technical challenge he had ever had. The story of David Holm, who is clubbed down in a graveyard on the stroke of midnight at the turn of the year, and who is resurrected by an embodiment of death (a coach-driver who emerges from the waves) to relive the crises and errors of his past existence, is narrated in a complex weave of flashbacks and superimpositions. For the sequence in the churchyard, everything had to be photographed at least twice. "We were proud of the ghosts' consistency," wrote Sjöström once the ticklish night shooting was over. "They were actually not flat and misty. As a result of artful lighting they had become three-dimensional in their spirituality."

Sjöström himself plays the role of David Holm with dazzling ease and without any makeup. As an actor, he is often limited by his own exuberance. He flings his entire personality into a scene, and thereby sacrifices his self-discipline. In *Thy Soul Shall Bear Witness,* he ranges from cynicism and wry humour to moments of agony and bewilderment. And the phantasmic scenes are even more credible because they are placed at intervals between the often brutally realistic incidents in the life of David Holm, the callous ribaldry in the taverns, and the harsh quarrels between husband and wife in front of the frightened children.

In 1923, Sjöström sailed for America, and an epoch was at an end. Unlike Stiller he made at least two masterpieces in Hollywood (*He Who Gets Slapped,* 1924 and *The Wind,* 1927), but they belong in another book, and to another time.

Mauritz Stiller

Mauritz Stiller, a Finn of Russian Jewish stock, whose career had paralleled Sjöström's in the early years of the century, took a little longer than Sjöström to win acclaim outside Sweden.

Stiller was suave, sophisticated and extremely musical. "He'd get physically sick when he saw anything ugly," recalled Sjöström later. To the world, he became famous during the 1920's as the mentor of Greta Garbo. Stiller was homosexual, and his relationship to Garbo was that of Pygmalion to Galatea. He never felt at home in Hollywood, and his star waned while Garbo's waxed. But during the 1910's and early 1920's he matched Sjöström stride for stride, and his films appear today to be far the livelier of the two directors'. If he ranks slightly below Sjöström in the Pantheon of world cinema, it may be because his work lacked the intensity of human passion that runs through that of his great colleague and rival.

In terms of personality the two men were as different as chalk and cheese. In fact, a wag might argue that had it not been for the pleasant euphony of their names in tandem, Sjöström and Stiller might never have been linked, no more than Renoir and Carné in the French cinema, or Reed and Lean in the British. Sjöström did of course act in certain Stiller pictures—although that was for contractual reasons more than anything else—and the two men did not mix socially. One cannot help feeling that the cosmopolitan Stiller may have secretly scoffed at

Sjöström, Garbo and Stiller in Hollywood during the mid-Twenties.

the stolid rural Swedishness of his colleague, but there is no evidence to prove it.

The differences are there for examination on screen. Although *The Black Masks* ("De svarta maskerna", 1912) astonished the fledgling industry with its assured use of parallel action and trick perspectives, it was not until *Love and Journalism* ("Kärlek och journalistik", 1916) that Stiller's personal style became apparent. His characters—a young female reporter, a polar explorer, a buxom housekeeper—are deftly-drawn, full of gusto and intelligence. The sexes skirmish, then retire to consider their next stratagem. But there is never the slightest hint of maliciousness in a Stiller situation: the lovers in his comedies are aware of their mutual attraction from the outset, but refuse to acknowledge defeat before they have shown their mettle. Each is ready, and secretly yearning, to enter an intimate, fantasy world. As Bengt Idestam-Almquist, the distinguished Swedish critic remarked: "As a director, Stiller was a Svengali, a torturing devil beyond compare, but he was loved by his sacrificial victims because he produced results."

Victor Sjöström and Karin Molander teamed together in a brace of masterly comedies by Stiller—*Thomas Graal's Best Film* ("Thomas Graals bästa film", 1917) and *Thomas Graal's First Child* ("Thomas Graals bästa barn", 1918). Graal is a famous scriptwriter who is infatuated with a secretary at the studios and concocts a scenario around her domestic life. Not only did this kind of plot prefigure such Hollywood triumphs as *Show People* (1928), but it demonstrates the truth of Ernst Lubitsch's own admission that he was influenced by Stiller. The profusion of visual gags never degenerates into slapstick or burlesque. The domestic relationships and the erotic byplay possess an application and a validity beyond their immediate setting and generation. Stiller's timing adds immeasurably to the comic effect of many sequences (for example, the quarrel on the honeymoon in the second film, when Thomas and Bessie withdraw to their respective bedrooms in high dudgeon, the two doors slammed in significant unison).

Erotikon (1920) lingers on as the most hallowed of Stiller's comedies, although its laughs are far more intermittent than those afforded by *Love and Journalism* or the *Thomas Graal* films. Still, the sheer scale of *Erotikon* exceeds anything that Sjöström would have dared to tackle. Its story of dalliance and infidelity in high places is so much fluff, vaguely portending such Bergman comedies as *Smiles of a Summer Night* or *All These Women* ("För att inte tala om alla dessa kvinnor", 1964), but Stiller did not hesitate to hire the opera house in Stockholm with 800 extras on scene; a ballet was composed for the film's most extravagant sequence; and more expense was lavished on scenes showing Tora Teje indulging in airplane excursions with her admirer. Not that such follies blunted the edge of Stiller's sarcastic wit. He did not so

17

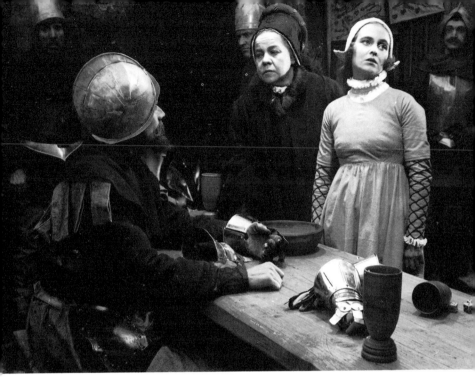

Mary Johnson as Elsalill in *Sir Arne's Treasure*.

much pillory as skewer the pretensions of the leisured classes in Swedish society. Yet he also admires the audacity of someone like Marthe, the niece of an old professor in the film, who throws contemporary modesty to the winds when she is alone, lights herself a cigarette and relaxes full-length on a couch with her calves amply exposed.

Johan (1921), based on a Finnish novel, stresses Stiller's profound grasp of the Nordic character and temperament. Fundamental to its theme is an idea that recurs again and again in Swedish cinema: a stranger represents a beacon of hope and excitement in the life of a remote community. Marit, a farmer's wife, is seduced by a passing visitor. He abducts her, and together they hurtle down a precipitous river, only to be caught by Marit's pursuing husband. The stranger is worsted but—and Stiller's understanding of human nature again comes to the fore—it is the farmer who is broken in spirit, for he realises that Marit did in fact leave of her own accord.

Stiller in this production matched Sjöström's description of pastoral life and physical labour. Nor could his colleague have surpassed the editing in the lovers' trip downstream, which appears as a continuous movement, a whirling descent into chaos and misadventure. So it is not surprising that three of Stiller's most monumental films should have been adapted from the work of Selma Lagerlöf who, though she probably preferred Sjöström as an individual, was forced to concede that Stiller was a master at recreating her world on screen.

Sir Arne's Treasure ("Herr Arnes penningar", 1919) is the greatest work in Stiller's career. Set in the 16th century, the film is blessed with the same historical authenticity as Bergman's *The Virgin Spring*—and the three mercenaries here have strong affinities with the rapists in the later picture. *Sir Arne's Treasure*, which chronicles the flight of three mercenaries from a castle, after a botched conspiracy during the reign of Johan III, is a tragedy in the fatalistic tradition of the Swedish cinema, but it also hints at psychological motives and effects in a far more mature manner than does most of Sjöström's work.

But *Sir Arne's Treasure* introduces another distinctive Stiller quality —his skill at integrating vision with reality. The crucial character of Elsalill (Mary Johnson), who alone survives the mercenaries' attack on Sir Arne's manor, relives the disaster over and over again. Her nightmares conflict with her steadily mounting love for Sir Archie, the good-looking dastardly leader of the Scottish mercenaries. This blighted romance is one of the most touching in all Swedish cinema, and no death is more poignant than that of Elsalill as, thrust forward like a shield by Sir Archie, she perishes on a soldier's lance. So the winding cortège across the ice at Marstrand brings Elsalill to her last resting-place, and constitutes one of the high points of Julius Jaenzon's career

Greta Garbo in *The Atonement of Gösta Berling*, the last film she made in Sweden before leaving for Hollywood.

as a cinematographer, comparable to Eisenstein and Tissé's images of the faithful coiling over the snow at the end of *Ivan the Terrible, Pt. I.*

Another spectacular film woven of dreams and reality, fears and idyllic fantasies, is *Gunnar Hedes Saga* or *The Old Mansion* ("Gunnar Hedes saga", 1922), a Lagerlöf tale that takes its meek, musician hero up to the northernmost reaches of Lapland, where he buys a herd of reindeer and drives them on the long trek south. An accident during a stampede nearly kills him, and he suffers amnesia. Mary Johnson is once more in her element as the girl who seeks to unlock her lover's mind, until finally the sound of her violin penetrates the darkness that has obscured his mind for so long. The film contains none of the sardonic tones that mark Stiller's comedies; rather it is the muted, spiritual ingredient already found in the less spectacular passages of *Sir Arne's Treasure* that predominates.

The Atonement of Gösta Berling ("Gösta Berlings saga", 1924) was intended to be the most glorious of all Swedish silent films up to that date. In the event, it was too cumbrous for its own good, and the flaws that crept in may be viewed now as the signals of decay in Swedish cinema. Although Greta Garbo as the young Italian girl who dotes on the handsome, defrocked parson, Gösta Berling, came to the fore in this production, there was a lack of zest and narrative flexibility quite astonishing in a director of Stiller's restlessness. The acting is over-emphatic, and scenes shot in the studios contrast painfully with those out of doors (particularly in the long chase across the ice, as Lars Hanson and Greta Garbo, aboard a large sled, try to outpace a pack of pursuing wolves).

However, when passing summary judgement on any of these remote films, one must bear in mind the quality of the materials to hand. Many of the original negatives and copies were destroyed by a fire at the Lidingö studios in the 1930's, and not even the most privileged historians have had the chance to view anything other than a fraction of the output of Sjöström and Stiller. There is no doubt that the impact their work made on contemporary critics and film-makers was considerable. More importantly, they established a living tradition that would fuel the inspiration of future film-makers like Alf Sjöberg, Ingmar Bergman and Jan Troell.

A golden era was at a close. Swedish films had triumphed not only in their own country but on the screens of numerous European countries—and in the United States, where even the movie moguls were impressed. Sjöström was invited to Hollywood, Garbo and Stiller were to follow soon afterwards, and the standards of Swedish camerawork were already legendary. In the dark days of the 1930's, when those who controlled Swedish studios had turned their backs on artistic aspirations, this entire silent period must have seemed like some vanished paradise.

Surviving the Thirties and Forties: the Quest for Commitment

Charles Magnusson was a great pioneering producer, but as early as 1920 his fire and flair began to diminish. He took for granted the prolific talents of Sjöström and Stiller, expecting a couple of films per season from each of them, with the result that in productions like *Master Man* ("Mästerman", 1920) and *The Surrounded House* ("Det omringade huset", 1923), Victor Sjöström's form was below par and he was not surprisingly tempted by an offer from the Goldwyn Studio to go to Hollywood (in 1923). Stiller, with his protégée Greta Garbo, followed two years later, and for a few brief years the Swedish cinema was transplanted to the sunstruck bungalows and backlots of Los Angeles.

The prominent financier, Ivar Kreuger, known during the 1920's as the Swedish "match king", had bought heavily into Svenska Bio even before it became Svensk Filmindustri (SF) in 1919. Share capital leapt from 2 million to 35 million Swedish kronor in less than eighteen months. Attractive new studios were built in the Stockholm suburb of Råsunda, and SF released the lion's share of the American films that now poured into the Scandinavian countries in the wake of the First World War.

Cinema as diversion

There were no gifted or uncompromising directors ready to follow in the footsteps of Stiller and Sjöström. Throughout the 1920's and 1930's, SF could offer to its film-makers the finest facilities, but with few exceptions the results were trite. When, in 1928, Magnusson was finally eased out of SF by Kreuger (who put his sidekick Olof Andersson in charge), Swedish cinema entered a barren period. In recent years there have been half-hearted attempts to rehabilitate the flood of so-called "pilsnerfilms" (like beer, all froth and no bite) but no neglected masterpieces have emerged, and the predominant genre – the sitcom – symbolised the isolationism of the local industry.

By the end of the 1920's a mood of conservatism had gripped the country. In the 1928 elections, Arvid Lindman's Conservative party gained 73 seats, and even though Carl G. Ekman assumed power at the head of the Liberals in June 1930, the depression could not be averted. Unemployment jumped from less than 50,000 in 1930 to 161,000 at the end of 1932. Kreuger's empire crashed about his ears, and he committed suicide at the end of 1932. The previous year, strikes had whipped up the traditionally calm waters of Swedish industrial relations (one such incident is recalled in Bo Widerberg's 1969 film, *The Ådalen Riots*).

So, as always happens in a time of economic recession or war, the public flocked to the cinemas. Diversion, not provocation, however, was required by the audiences. A film like *Ingeborg Holm* would have failed utterly in 1932; instead, spectators craved fluff like *Love and the Home Guard* ("Kärlek och landstorm", 1931), *Love and Deficit* ("Kärlek och kassabrist", 1932) and *The Southsiders* ("Söderkåkar", 1932). Such films, hastily grasping at the gimmickry of sound, could beguile the public with trivial dialogue or innocuous songs. The studios maintained a steady production output of around 25 features per annum, and nearly everyone was content.

When discussing films from this era one should not forget the modest achievements of popular players such as Fridolf Rhudin (a Swedish Buster Keaton who died in mid-decade); Edvard Persson, whose Scanian accent and folksy patriotic fervour endeared his lumpish figure to a whole generation of Swedish filmgoers; and of course those two symbols of Nordic beauty who were quick to respond to the lure of the Hollywood studios – Ingrid Bergman and Signe Hasso.

Some directors did seek to rise above the dross. In 1929 Alf Sjöberg, who had made a considerable impact with his stage work at the Royal Dramatic Theatre during the mid-1920's, recorded a startling debut in the cinema with *The Strongest* ("Den starkaste"), a tale of seal-hunters in the Greenland Sea and their seasonal return to a tranquil Sound and the farmlands around it. Human rivalries and jealousies are played out in the weird, snowy landscape. Gustaf, the handsome stranger, woos Ingeborg from under the nose of stolid Ole, but to the end he remains a chivalrous figure, relishing the continual struggle with nature and her demands far more than the duel with Ole over the girl at home. Man versus the elements is indeed the major theme of Sjöberg's film. "Here," says the old father, "right belongs to the strongest." One is back in the primitive environment of *The Outlaw and His Wife*. Sjöberg is obviously in debt to Sjöström in so far as the landscape dominates the action, but he brings to the style of the film a sophistication far superior to that of the witless comedies that were to strangle Swedish cinema in the 1930's.

The likes of Sjöberg were not welcome, however, at the studios in the era's prevailing mood of flippancy, and a full decade would elapse before Sjöberg could again direct a picture.

Gustaf Molander

Gustaf Molander, whose screenplays for Sjöström and Stiller had contributed to the brilliance of the early silent period in Swedish cinema, was year by year maturing into the father figure of the industry. He directed 14 films during the 1920's, and no less than 22 in the ensuing ten years. Most of them have vanished into oblivion, but at least three deserve mention. *One Night* ("En natt", 1931) was a drama set in Finland, at the time of the revolution that resulted in Finnish independence from Russia in 1917. Molander's use of sound effects was intelligent, and his grasp of the political issues involved was rare for 1931. But his greatest success came in tandem with the Swedish cinema's foremost icon of that time—the actor Gösta Ekman. The family study, *Swedenhielms* (1935), and the triangle romance, *Intermezzo* (1936), were ideal vehicles for Ekman's passionate, would-be tragic style of acting, an idiom more suited to the stage than to the intimacy of the film set.

In *Swedenhielms* he makes a delightful entrance, creeping through the front door to surprise his family beneath a broad-brimmed hat. A

Ingrid Bergman and
Gösta Ekman
in *Intermezzo*.

scientist whose glorious career cannot lessen the *tristesse* of his private
life, Ekman is most impressive in solo scenes—when, for example, he
gazes piteously up at his wife's portrait, and then returns to his arm-
chair, a bowed figure, and turns out the light for the sake of peace. The
family characters remind us that the film springs full-blown from the
frivolous 1930's. Young Swedenhielm is in financial straits, as is the
housekeeper's favourite son. These spoilt young men complain about
the decline in their standard of living. Ingrid Bergman is the only
relaxed member of the household, making gentle fun of her lieutenant
beau even when he pretends to have fallen out of love with her.

Intermezzo is a child of its epoch too. Today, its saccharine romance
between a great violinist and his children's young music teacher (Ingrid

Bergman), can be treated with all the disdain reserved for high camp. Some pulse still throbs at the heart of this eager film, however. Perhaps it is Gösta Ekman's impassioned conviction as the happily-married husband who tries so hard to wring a second chance from life. Perhaps it is Ingrid Bergman's unforced devotion as the shy young teacher, distraught at the domestic schism she has caused. The moral guilt of the period adds a dark overtone to the film, with the photograph of the maestro's daughter always close to him.

In the 1940's, directors seemed more committed to reflecting social change and with Swedish cinema again a respectable medium, Molander could once more afford to tackle risky topics. *Ride Tonight* ("Rid i natt!", 1942) proved to be a disturbing paradigm for what was happening in Nazi Germany; set during the Thirty Years' War, *Ride Tonight!* caught admirably the denunciation of totalitarianism explicit in Vilhelm Moberg's novel, while at the same time re-creating the atmosphere of 17th century Sweden with an eye for historical verisimilitude that seemed to characterise the early 1940's (Sjöberg's *The Road to Heaven* and *The Royal Hunt* are similarly impressive). The passive resistance of country folk to the ravages of the Swedish nobility became a symbol of the anti-Fascist mood in neutral Sweden during the Hitler period. Molander also dealt with contemporary issues in *There Burned a Flame* ("Det brinner en eld", 1943), which focused on the effects of the German occupation of Oslo.

Molander's career, seemingly inexhaustible, continued for another two decades, although perhaps the only three films of which he could be proud during that time were scripted by the neophyte Ingmar Bergman: *Woman without a Face* ("Kvinna utan ansikte", 1947), *Eva* (1948), and *Divorced* ("Frånskild", 1951). Feelings of guilt and anguish, and the ultimate sanction of suicide, troubled the bland surface of Molander's direction in all these productions.

Back to earth—socio-political themes start to emerge
Swedish film did not remain entirely oblivious to outside tendencies even during the 1930's, as demonstrated by the repellent anti-Semitism

of films like *Panic* (implying that Kreuger's collapse was engineered by Jewish financiers) and Per-Axel Branner's *Pettersson & Bendel* (1933), skilful though the latter was—Hans Alfredson produced a conspicuously different "remake" in 1984. The existentialism that would percolate the European consciousness during the 1940's was already evident in films like *A Crime* ("Ett brott", 1940), in which Anders Henrikson charted the rebellion of a judge's son against an older generation, and particularly against the hallowed concept of the nuclear family (Sjöberg would deal another severe blow to this bastion in *Iris and The Lieutenant),* and *They Staked Their Lives* ("Med livet som insats", 1939), with its overriding sense of catastrophe as the harassed members of an underground resistance movement seek to combat the rigours of an unidentified Nordic "police" state. Sjöberg directed this film with the same adroitness and self-confidence that he had exhibited in *The Strongest,* which made his enforced absence from the studios all the more regrettable. Already Sjöberg was able to treat the film medium on its own terms, eschewing theatrical conventions in favour of a more urgent rhythm, a better balance between close-up conversations and action observed in long-shot. The frequent quarrels among the agents, and their melancholy gatherings in bare rooms, emphasise Sjöberg's fatalism and the perplexities of a Europe drifting inexorably into conflict.

In 1932, Per Albin Hansson's Social Democrats took office, and for the next 44 years Swedish government was to be controlled by the Social Democrats. Although Hansson and his visionary Minister of Finance, Ernst Wigforss, set in train several vital reforms during the 1930's there was still much to be done in the ensuing decade, and Swedish society only underwent a fundamental change during the war years. Gradually the Swedish cinema began to monitor this social upheaval. Directors such as Hampe Faustman and Alf Sjöberg—and to a limited extent also Hasse Ekman—attempted to spotlight the injustices, irrelevancies, and discriminatory aspects of Swedish life.

Faustman was the fiercest in his condemnation of the class society. Reared on the Soviet cinema, and admiring Mark Donskoi in particular, he based each of his major works on the struggle between freedom and tyranny. He sympathised with the lot of Swedish farm labourers in *When Meadows Bloom* ("När ängarna blommar", 1946), a film that resembles the first postwar productions from Eastern Europe (Frigyes Bán's *The Soil under Your Feet,* for example). He uses the classical situation of a strike on which to construct the film. The landowner, with his Alsatian dog and feathered hat, stands as a symbol of intolerance and ruthless authority. The agricultural workers huddle together in restless groups, congregating in their leader's cabin to hear a record of the "Internationale", or, like Birger Malmsten (who would become well-known in Bergman's early films), casting quick glances in the direction of the boss's daughter.

Faustman's commitment and defiance are unashamed, rejecting the clichés of 1940's cinema. He shared the horror of contemporary writers when confronted with the horrors of Nazism and the lethal prospects engendered by the atomic bomb, but he still sought after humanistic ideals. *Foreign Harbour* ("Främmande hamn", 1948) deals with the clandestine shipment of arms to the Fascists, an abuse of neutrality that must have stung a government which had turned a blind eye to the Bofors gun and to the trundling of trains by night through the country en route to Denmark and Norway, bearing arms. The action of the film takes place in the small Polish harbour of Gdynia (although exteriors were shot in Finland), and Faustman's skill at chronicling the life of the docks and the ship's crew is masterly. High-angle shots look down on the men in their cramped quarters and emphasise the sordidness of their plight as they scrabble like animals in the snow for potato peelings. The encroaching ice is always in the background, cutting off the crew's retreat from their misery and isolating the harbour itself so that the central issue—should or should not the cargo be accepted—is inescapable.

Other important films by Faustman include *God and the Gipsyman* ("Gud fader och tattaren", 1954) which, like many novels of the period, espoused the cause of the gipsies in their efforts to achieve recognition from society; *Night in the Harbour* ("Natt i hamn, 1943), in which Gunnar Fischer made his early mark as a cinematographer; and *U-båt 39* (1952), an adaption of the controversial play by Rudolf Värnlund, which had been staged in Stockholm by the young Ingmar Bergman at the height of the war .

Newcomers to the Forties scene

The revival of the Swedish cinema in the early 1940's was due in part to the appointment of Carl Anders Dymling to the stewardship of SF. A scholar in his own right, and also a first-class administrator (he had been head of the Swedish Radio), Dymling was quick to encourage new talent, even if it meant risking money. He also appointed Victor Sjöström as "Artistic Director", who in turn would encourage the young Ingmar Bergman when he was working on his first independent feature, *Crisis,* in 1945.

Among those who began their career soon after Dymling's arrival was Arne Sucksdorff, whose nature documentaries became famous well beyond the borders of Sweden. His work is symptomatic of that recurrent Swedish preoccupation with the passage of the seasons, while individual films such as *The Gull* ("Trut!", 1944) made an oblique comment on the Nazi mentality and violence it excited. The struggle for survival in wartime conditions was an everyday reality for most Europeans apart from the Swedes and the Swiss, and in Sucksdorff's camera eye the clash between the strong and the weak in nature took on a metaphorical tinge. Even in one of his most gentle documentaries, the impressionistic *Rhythm of a City* ("Människor i stad", 1947), Stockholm becomes a place where the fittest survive best. One boy snatches a football from another and dashes away through the uneven streets of the Old Town, while in conclusion there is the spectacle of a blind man fumbling for his violin bow on the cobbles.

A Divided World ("En kluven värld", 1948) marks a return to the forest. The winter snow gleams in the moonlight. The trees are still, and cast mysterious shadows over the valley. And while the hunt for food progresses, the notes of a Bach Fantasia are heard soaring from the organ of a nearby church. A fox cub traps a hare, only to have the

Arne Sucksdorff.

A Divided World.

carcass snatched away from him by an owl. As always, Sucksdorff's analysis of the order of nature is relentlessly accurate.

Hasse Ekman

Hasse Ekman, the son of the celebrated Gösta, and father in his turn of yet another popular Gösta Ekman, was much in demand as both actor and director during the early 1940's. An arch if friendly rival to Ingmar Bergman, he matched him in his direction of players and brought to his first few films a deftness of touch that Bergman would not equal until the 1950's. Most of these productions have faded from sight, however, and ironically Ekman is recognised by today's generation of film buffs as nothing more than the simpering Frans in Bergman's *Sawdust and Tinsel/The Naked Night*. There remain moments to savour, though, in *First Division* ("Första divisionen", 1941), with its cheerful, propagandist image of the Swedish Air Force during wartime, neutral though Sweden was; in *Changing Trains* ("Ombyte av tåg", 1943), astonishingly precursive of *Brief Encounter* in its tender and elegiac story of transient happiness between two young people at a railway station; *The Banquet* ("Banketten", 1948), a bitter indictment of the degeneracy of the Swedish aristocracy; and *Girl with Hyacinths* ("Flicka och hyacinter", 1950), with its kaleidoscopic reconstruction of a young woman's life — and death. There are few more poignant cases of suicide in the Swedish cinema than that of Dagmar Brink in this latter work by Ekman. To a conspicuous degree Dagmar is the conscience of a neutral Sweden, and the spiritual depression that pervaded the intelligentsia in the immediate postwar years. Only perhaps in *Girl with Hyacinths* did Ekman bid fair to establish a recognisable world of his own. For the most part, his work is that of a journeyman technician such as Michael Curtiz in Hollywood.

Alf Sjöberg

Alf Sjöberg demonstrated throughout his career that it was not a prerequisite of international success to create a familiar set of characters and dramatic situations, as Bergman was to do so brilliantly. For a start,

Girl with Hyacinths with Birgit Tengroth and Eva Henning.

Sjöberg was much more the professional trouper than was Bergman, who railed against the conventions of the film studios and tended to upset just about everyone with whom he came in contact in his prentice years.

Sjöberg, like Marcel Carné in occupied France, resolved to comment on the disturbing issues of the present through the device of setting his art in the past. Like Carné too, he brought to the cinema the intelligent lighting and flamboyant performances of the theatre. *The Royal Hunt* ("Kungajakt", 1943) paints a vivid canvas of 18th century life, rich in intrigue and patriotic exuberance. Russian efforts to unseat Gustaf III

Alf Sjöberg.

are met with resistance by those loyal to the crown, and Sjöberg evokes the extremes of the period with panache in his opening sequences, with a duel being fought beneath a bright afternoon sun and the patronising eyes of the courtiers, and then a tavern brawl set in motion by night, with gnarled faces looming out of the smoke and the shadows.

More cohesive by far was *The Road to Heaven* ("Himlaspelet", 1942), part allegory, part fantasy, that at once harked back to the silent films of Lagerlöf/Sjöström, and became a precedent for Bergman's great morality, *The Seventh Seal*. Credit for the concept and allegorical strength of the film must go to Rune Lindström, who had written *The Road to Heaven* while at the University of Uppsala studying to be a

Eva Dahlbeck in *Only a Mother*.

parson. Ever since, it has been performed almost every year in the small town of Leksand on Lake Silja, in the heart of the Dalecarlian district it celebrates. Mats Ersson is a young, naive peasant who is incensed by the unjust trial and condemnation of his fiancée Marit as a witch. After she has been burned at the stake, Mats strides off on "the road to heaven", to demand justice and recompense. His inspiration comes from the murals in the local church (those quaint compositions so familiar to the tourist from reproductions in books and on textiles), and Mats marches along the country ways to the stirring accompaniment of folk-song and ditty. Like any idealist, however, and like those at bay before the Nazi threat, Mats succumbs to the Devil's blandishments. He drinks and fornicates, grows rich on a chance discovery of copper ore, and is only saved on his deathbed by the Good Father, who has observed him from the outset of his long journey towards heaven. Mats tries desperately to justify his selfishness, and distributes all his gold. Then, prompted by the implacable reasoning of the Good Father, he recalls the lofty aims of his original pilgrimage. "No one is strong enough," says Mary, the Magdalene figure, as Mats admits his weakness. "Poor Mats, you were a straw in the wind." At last he dies, and finds himself awakening in flower-laden meadows, with his long-lost fiancée waiting to embrace him.

Some scenes in *The Road to Heaven* rank with the finest ever achieved by a Swedish film-maker: the headlong dash across the plain to the City of Desire, with Mats riding a horse-drawn sleigh with uninhibited glee, or the final, poignant encounter of Mats and the mistress he had met on his travels. This happy conjunction of Bunyanesque piety and pastoral contentment holds *The Road to Heaven* in a delicate balance. Sjöberg's often theatrical compositions are more charming than tedious.

Apart from *Frenzy* (see next chapter), Sjöberg's output during the 1940's was distinguished by two other excellent films—*Iris and The Lieutenant* ("Iris och löjtnantshjärta", 1946), a love story featuring the young Mai Zetterling and Alf Kjellin that plunged a romantic dagger into the heart of the patriarchal society then being replaced by the more egalitarian conditions of the Social Democratic government; and *Only a Mother* ("Bara en mor", 1949), with its gutsy, wholesome performance by Eva Dahlbeck as the labouring farm-hand who is swept remorselessly to her death by successive pregnancies and a daily burden of physical toil. Sjöberg in this latter work condemns the system, not the rhythm, of bucolic life. Like so many of his films, it pricked the conscience of a country still emerging from a 19th century code of class and conduct.

The Rise of Ingmar Bergman

Ingmar Bergman devoted his formative years to the theatre even more intensively than he did to the cinema. The early 1940's was a fruitful period in the development of Swedish stage production. Per Lindberg, who had studied under Max Reinhardt and whose slender output of films—*The Norrtull Gang* ("Norrtullsligan", 1923), *The Old Man's Coming* ("Gubben kommer", 1939) and *June Night* ("Juninatten", 1940)—possessed an offbeat quality, was to a considerable degree responsible for the concept and design of Malmö City Theatre, which opened its doors in 1944. Bergman would spend some of his most glorious years exploring the resources of this superb auditorium.

There were strong links between stage and screen at this period. Vilhelm Moberg's *Ride Tonight!* was premiered in Stockholm in September 1942, just two months before Gustaf Molander's film version opened. Most of the creative directors in Sweden were involved in the theatre, among them Alf Sjöberg, while the stage critic Herbert Grevenius became a screenwriter for Bergman and the artistic director at the Göteborg City Theatre, Torsten Hammarén, would become a crucial mentor to the fledgling genius during the latter years of the decade.

Bergman's apprentice years

Much of Bergman's work of the 1940's no longer withstands close scrutiny. He was eager to grasp at whatever assignment might come his way, using B-movie material on which to whittle his abrasive talent to a fine cutting edge. The irony and despair of his early scripts echo to some extent the work of the so-called Fortyists, a group of writers including Stig Dagerman and Erik Lindegren; but Bergman offered an extra dimension—a visual flair that grew increasingly bold as the years went by. The eponymous anti-hero of this prentice phase in Bergman's

Mai Zetterling in *Frenzy* (1944).

career is a down-at-heel bohemian, rejected by the authorities and the bourgeois majority, and yet scorned by the intellectuals. Incarnated by such axiomatic performers as Stig Olin and Birger Malmsten, these often incoherent personalities provided the central driving force of otherwise drab and pompous films like *Crisis* ("Kris", 1945), *It Rains on Our Love* ("Det regnar på vår kärlek", 1946), *A Ship Bound for India* or *Land of Desire,* as it is also known ("Skepp till Indialand", 1947), and *Music in Darkness* ("Musik i mörker", 1947).

Bergman was fortunate, however, in finding Svensk Filmindustri keen to produce his screenplay, *Frenzy* ("Hets") in 1944. Alf Sjöberg agreed to direct the film (released in the United States as *Torment*), and worked on the script, developing its anti-Nazi motif, so that the story of a sadistic schoolmaster who inflicts humiliation on a senior schoolboy and his girlfriend (an experience Bergman himself had suffered during the 1930's) became a gripping paradigm for the oppressive regime in Germany. Stig Järrel, who played the teacher, Caligula, resembled Himmler with his smooth sophistry and steel-rimmed spectacles. As the young girl forced into a life of prostitution, Mai Zetterling introduced a streak of raw emotion into a hitherto refined tradition of Swedish female acting, and soon afterwards was placed under contract by the Rank Organisation in Britain.

Bergman has often been criticised—especially by the younger generations of Swedish film-makers—for ignoring the realities of the society round about him, for being too concerned with man's relationship to God or to his personal conscience. By an ironic paradox, this very quality has enabled Bergman to capture a worldwide audience while most of the committed directors of the 1960's and 1970's have remained penned within the Nordic area as far as distribution and appreciation of their work have been concerned. Bergman's fantasy and his comprehension of human foibles have proved more engaging than social diatribe.

From time to time, however, Bergman has anchored his films in a radical context, while avoiding allegiance to a particular political party or group. In 1948, for example, his *Port of Call* ("Hamnstad") not only offered a realistic picture of life in one of Scandinavia's busiest cities (Gothenburg), but also contained a scathing critique of the official line on abortion. At root, of course, Bergman is more interested in the personal relationships—between Gösta, the seaman who has hitherto lurched cheerfully from woman to woman, and Berit, the miserable girl who tries to commit suicide and is rescued by Gösta. Although his own parents were not in the habit of quarrelling in front of their children, Ingmar Bergman has always dramatised and verbalised the conflicts between husband and wife. In *Port of Call,* Berit's mother and father bicker and taunt each other while retaining the illusion of enjoying a happy life together. By comparison, Bergman recalls how his father, a clergyman who rose to become Chaplain to the Royal Court of Sweden, would sit with his wife at the dinner table, where they would "talk to each other in a nice, controlled way, but you felt the whole time that there was an enormous tension between them, an enormous aggression." Bergman's need to shock, to assault the viewer with violent or taboo imagery, stems from the repression of his home.

The distinctive visual flair for which Bergman became famous did not manifest itself until the late 1940's, in *Prison* ("Fängelse", 1948) and *Thirst* ("Törst", 1949). *Prison* was based on an original screenplay of Bergman's and demonstrated his ability to fuse past and present, dream and actuality, while touching on the themes that would become familiar in the years ahead. A supercilious young film director (Hasse Ekman) is visited by his old maths teacher, while out at the studios shooting a new production. The professor explains his idea for a film: it would revolve around Hell and the Devil, based on the notion that Hell exists on earth and that the Devil wields unlimited power over human lives. The director mentions this obviously unfilmable scheme to a journalist friend (played by Birger Malmsten), who plunges without delay into the recesses of Stockholm's Old Town in search of the heroine for such a movie. She is Birgitta Carolina, a hapless creature whose ruthless protector forces her into prostitution. Like Bertha in *Frenzy,* Birgitta Carolina finds solace in the arms of a social outsider, Thomas, but in the end she takes her own life.

The structure of *Prison* leaves much to be desired but, as a kind of melting-pot for Bergman's still inchoate ideas and fancies, it is a fascinating source for the film student. Bergman achieved his effects on a shoestring budget. Working for Lorens Marmstedt at Terrafilm, he brought the production in for only 240,000 kronor (some 20% cheaper than the norm for the time), and declared in a newspaper interview just before the premiere that these constraints had been an advantage: "Do an inexpensive film, do the cheapest film ever made in a Swedish studio, and you get the freedom to create according to your own con-

Birger Malmsten and Doris Svedlund in *Prison*.

science and desires." Bergman made do without extras, he pared the music to a minimum, shot his exteriors without elaborate lights or sound recording, started work earlier than normal each morning, and squeezed all his rehearsals into the actual shooting schedule. Bengt Idestam-Almquist, writing in "Stockholms-Tidningen", waxed enthusiastic: "For the first time in 25 years, Sweden is again at the head of world film development." He singled out Bergman's genuine *feeling* for images, although other critics found *Prison* reminiscent of the worst excesses of German expressionism.

Thirst, although derived from a collection of short stories by the pessimistic novelist Birgit Tengroth (who also played a supporting role in the film), laid bare the quivering, vulnerable surface of Bergman's psyche even more effectively than *Prison*. It emphasised the spiritual debt he owed to Strindberg, whose couples were also fettered by scorn and bitterness, as well as by an arid physical yearning for one another. In *Thirst*, Rut (played by Eva Henning) and her husband Bertil are returning from a holiday in southern Europe. Their journey, like all journeys in Bergman's world, proves to be a time of discovery and self-analysis. The hunger and strife signified by the sights that confront Rut and Bertil through the window of their train compartment are but reflections of the couple's inner turmoil. At one station, crowds beg for food; and the silhouette of bomb-ravaged buildings by night suggests the legacy of war, a vague cosmic event that Bergman has always related to personal issues.

Loneliness is the antagonist of many an early Bergman character. In *Thirst*, there are two specific forms of loneliness: that devouring Rut, as she sits trapped in her train compartment with a well-meaning but insensitive husband, and that encroaching on Viola (Birgit Tengroth) as she wanders distraught through the deserted streets of Stockholm on Midsummer's Eve. Viola was for a while Bertil's mistress, so there is a tenuous connection between the couples. Far from irritating the viewer, however, this second female personality serves to illuminate one of Bergman's most remarkable talents—his understanding of women and their emotional constitution. Indeed, Bergman's male figures are almost invariably dull and crass into the bargain, often pompous and seldom skilful lovers. The women in these early films may be shrewish and self-assertive, fickle and even rapacious, but they excite Bergman's admiration.

Although Eva Henning's pugnacious performance as Rut in *Thirst* is outstanding of its kind, the first of Bergman's major actress discoveries was Maj-Britt Nilsson, in *To Joy* ("Till glädje", 1950) and *Summer Interlude* ("Sommarlek", 1951). The egocentric violinist (played by Stig Olin) in *To Joy* is the last of Bergman's young artists to figure prominently in his cinema—although throughout his career the entertainer as such has been a butt for society's contempt. *To Joy*, which suggests that true love is more significant than a career, still ends with the triumph of music over marriage, and the film's interludes of sunshine (summer holidays in the Stockholm archipelago) are enhanced by a performance of wisdom and dignity by Victor Sjöström, then already 70 years of age, as the conductor of the Helsingborg Orchestra.

Two masters emerge

During the postwar period, Bergman had been consolidating his reputation as a stage director, first in Helsingborg, and later in Gothenburg. When, in 1952, he was appointed fulltime director and artistic adviser at Malmö City Theatre, he brought some of the actors and actresses who had worked with him on stage and screen. Yet Bergman would rarely fall into the trap of producing mere "filmed theatre", as did Sjöberg in his final phase.

The 1950's began with both these major Swedish directors at the very peak of their form. Bergman produced *Summer Interlude* while almost simultaneously, in the summer of 1950, Sjöberg was making *Miss Julie,* a film that would earn him the Palme d'Or in Cannes the following year.

At first glance a sentimental romance, based in fact on one of the adolescent Bergman's first brushes with love, *Summer Interlude* subtly inverts traditional sexual roles. Here it is the young woman, Marie, who pursues a busy career as a ballerina attached to the Opera in Stockholm. Henrik, her boyfriend, appears to have no "occupation" whatever, and carries round with him a delicate white poodle, treating it with the same care and affection as a young mother would lavish on her baby. While Marie is sturdy, decisive, and sweats away at her barre exercises, Henrik gives an impression of hesitancy and languor, two traits habitually associated with women.

The central skein of flashbacks, to a glorious summer in the archipelago, with Marie meeting Henrik and running with him the whole gamut of first love's aches and pleasures, revealed a lyrical side to Bergman's personality as a film-maker. Set like adversaries against these pastoral compositions are the scenes backstage at the Opera, where Marie unwinds in her dressing room and endures the taunts of the ballet-master (Stig Olin), who senses her discomfort and tells her that she dares neither to remove her makeup nor to leave it on—in short that she cannot bear to relinquish the past or bring herself to accept the present. The bald facts are that Henrik died by accident when diving off some rocks, and that now a scruffy, cynical journalist is lining up for Marie's favours. When she peels away her false eyelashes with a slow, deliberate movement, it is as though she were stripping the layer of artificiality that has obscured her soul since the death of Henrik.

Another sign of Bergman's maturity is his treatment of the supporting roles in *Summer Interlude:* the ballet-master, grotesque in his own makeup from *Coppelia,* Marie's uncle Erland, a noxious, disenchanted relic of the prewar haute bourgeoisie with whom Bergman's family had once mixed, the old lady, dying of cancer, who cares for Henrik on the island and plays chess with the local parson and Kaj, the world-weary ballerina whose refusal to maintain appearances contrasts with Marie's own decorum. Each of these characters springs to life in a few lines and images, giving a depth of field to the film's central relationship.

Like *To Joy, Summer Interlude* ends on a note of affirmation, to the sound of classical music. In each film, the leading personality has found "the joy that is beyond suffering and comprehension." Art for Bergman is cathartic; it is the touchstone of life, rising above questions of morality and public responsibility.

Miss Julie ("Fröken Julie", 1950) based on the play by Strindberg about the Count's daughter who seduces the footman and then commits suicide, also attempts to purge the past of its guilt and inhibition. *Miss Julie* stemmed from Strindberg's own experience in being coveted by Siri von Essen—a Countess while he professed to be the son of a servant girl—and proved a bitter diatribe against a class system that has long disappeared in Sweden. While the play takes place exclusively within the bounds of a large kitchen below stairs in the Count's mansion, Sjöberg's film ranges out and about on this fateful Midsummer's Eve, and also re-creates the traumatic incidents from Miss Julie's childhood. But he never allows his lovers to escape entirely from the present: the

44

black-caped governess, for example, chases the young Jean through the park and suddenly bursts into the same frame as Jean and Miss Julie *in the present.* And again, Miss Julie sits musing in the lofty salon while the image she recalls—of her mother carrying her in her arms—appears directly behind her.

Humiliation runs like a raw filigree through each major scene of *Miss Julie.* Jean as a man is mocked by Miss Julie in front of the crowd at the barn-dance: Jean as a boy is humiliated by the governess, and then beaten by his father. Miss Julie herself administers a public spanking to her fiancé during a ride in the park; while in one of the final memories in the film her mother harshly forbids her as a child to retain her beloved doll.

This masterpiece carries a powerful surge of erotic energy beneath the elegant decorum of its imagery. The Midsummer's pole is erected by the lusty crowd of retainers like some monstrous phallus. At the height of the dancing, guns are heard firing, and a close-up of a barrel shows wine gushing out like sperm. Miss Julie yearns for Jean to place his revolver in her mouth, while the killing of her pet greenfinch is an act of release for Jean, symbolically implying his own castration, and thus freedom at last from desire for his mistress.

The international acclaim for *Miss Julie* not only injected new vigour into Sjöberg's screen career, but also spotlit the superb ensemble acting that seemed to be at the Swedish cinema's beck and call. Much of the explanation could be found in the tradition of actors working on stage during the long Scandinavian winter months, and then swelling their income by appearing in films in those few sunlit weeks of summer when shooting tends to take place in Sweden. Anita Björk, as Miss Julie, and Ulf Palme, as Jean, were among the most persuasive players of their generation, but right down the cast list may be found some of Sweden's brightest names of stage and screen—Anders Henrikson as the Count, Margaretha Krook as the governess, Åke Fridell as Robert, and a young Max von Sydow as the drunken groom.

Sjöberg and Bergman now matched each other film for film. During the next three years, Bergman's output included *Summer with Monika,*

Anita Björk in the title role of *Miss Julie*.

Waiting Women, Sawdust and Tinsel, A Lesson in Love, and *Journey into Autumn,* while Sjöberg, in what may be seen with hindsight as a final surge of creative zest, produced *Barabbas, Karin Månsdotter,* and the underestimated *Wild Birds.*

Ingmar Bergman

Bergman and his crew spent the long hot summer of 1952 on the island of Ornö, shooting *Summer with Monika* ("Sommaren med Monika"), a story of infatuation and disillusionment that was perfectly wedded to the climatic dictates of the Swedish year: uninhibited sex in the archipelago beneath a cloudless sky, then the return to Stockholm as the winds of autumn gather strength, and an affair turning sour. Harriet Andersson, flaunting her physical charms without pretensions or thought for the future, emerged from the film not only as a ready-made star, but also as Bergman's companion for the next few years, accompanying him to Malmö and acting in his ensuing four screen productions. She was set apart from other leading Swedish actresses by the bluntness and naturalism of her approach to life. Her minx-like mien appealed to older men, as Bergman perceived when casting her as the circus-owner's mistress in *Sawdust and Tinsel/The Naked Night* ("Gycklarnas afton", 1953) and as the romantic ideal of Gunnar Björnstrand's aging Consul in *Journey into Autumn* or *Dreams* ("Kvinnodröm", 1955). Her zest for life illuminates these otherwise sombre films, filled with the bitter taste of love betrayed and age at the mercy of youth, in the circus ring or in the struggle for affection.

Neither the established name of Sjöberg nor the fast-increasing reputation of Bergman were sufficient, however, to gurarantee box-office success. Sjöberg's films after *Miss Julie* lost huge sums for their producers, and Bergman's *Sawdust and Tinsel* flopped disastrously outside Stockholm. All this was a blow to Sandrew's admirable young producer, Rune Waldekranz, whose belief in *Sawdust and Tinsel* has been vindicated with the passing years. Imaginative producers in Sweden have been conspicuous by their rarity: Waldekranz, a respected film historian, was one of the best at this period. At Svensk Filmindustri, Carl Anders Dymling would prove to be the pillar behind Ingmar Bergman's international career, placing his faith in a director whose track record left much to be desired, in commercial terms.

Sawdust and Tinsel has emerged as one of Bergman's authentic masterpieces, fierce in its attack on male chauvinism, fatalistic in its vision of the entertainer doomed to cavort before a crass and sadistic audience. The bitterness in this film welled up from Bergman's own experience as a director in Sweden, but the brilliant technique proved that this man of 35 was at last a master of his art. No anthology of European cinema would be complete without the opening sequence from *Sawdust*

Harriet Andersson and Åke Grönberg in a scene from *Sawdust and Tinsel.*

and Tinsel. Shot in harsh, chalky white long-shots and close-ups, it narrates a terrifying allegory, as the circus clown is humiliated by his flirtacious wife, and must drag her on his back from the seashore, like Christ staggering over the pitiless stones on his way to Golgotha.

Journey into Autumn, unrelieved by such dazzling set-pieces, and set moreover in a drab modern city, is even more sombre in tone. Yet the film possesses a haunting mood of its own, an unostentatious melancholy perfectly embodied in the character of the Consul, who buys pearls and fine clothes for the young fashion model he meets in the street, and who reminds him of a wife long incarcerated in a mental home. Rhyming with this winter's tale is a more conventional affair, between a married man and his mistress from Stockholm; the romance between them has ebbed away, and when the man's wife surprises the couple in a hotel room, there ensues one of Bergman's characteristically stinging monologues, mocking and vilifying the sexual transgressors.

Alf Sjöberg

Alf Sjöberg had staged several of the plays of Pär Lagerkvist over the years, and seized the opportunity to make a film from his *Barabbas* (1952). He spent more than two months shooting on locations in Israel and Italy, but although the production bore all the hallmarks of a prestige presentation, Anders Sandrew must have bitterly regretted his decision to refuse Louis B. Mayer's offer to buy the rights, so as to remake the film in the United States, with Spencer Tracy as Barabbas. The critical response to the first screenings at the Cannes Festival of 1953 was appalling, and foreign sales amounted to a fraction of what Sandrews had anticipated.

The plot, which traces the expiation of his guilt through suffering by Barabbas in the months following the death of Christ, contains much colourful incident. The scenes in the copper mines of Cyprus, for example, and the great fire of Rome in which Barabbas is swept up, are described with considerable panache. But Sjöberg was more at home dealing with the life of another misunderstood figure from history—the Swedish king, Erik XIV—in *Karin Månsdotter* (1954). Where Ulf Palme as Barabbas had been leaden-footed and humourless, Jarl Kulle as the mad monarch of the Nordic Middle Ages positively sparkled with energy and manic glee. Palme himself contributed a solid portrait of Erik's statesman, Göran Persson, but while Sjöberg's narrative often sags between bursts of action, the character of the King never flags. He veers from euphoria to despair, leaping like some panic-stricken gazelle up and down the broad winding staircases of his castle. He takes as mistress the 14-year-old peasant girl, Karin Månsdotter, loses her through his cruelty and neglect, and in a final tender scene in her father's hut, is reconciled with her.

49

In Sjöberg's personal films, men and women are led by their instincts and respond to temptations. They are anxious not be affected by social conventions. *Wild Birds* ("Vildfåglar", 1955) was yet another fiasco for the director, and yet its stereotyped characters inhabit a milieu brought sharply to life by the cinematography, *mise en scène,* and editing. The young sailor, Nisse Bortom, resembles Gösta in *Port of Call,* a quick prey to liquor and susceptible to decent girls. The film contains an orgy scene that the censor tried to cut, without success, before the film's premiere. The naked sexuality of the dancing is emphasised by Sjöberg's cross-cutting between the dance and a fist-fight between two men in a corner of the room.

The tragedy of Alf Sjöberg's career as a film-maker was that he could not develop his characters from year to year. His sympathy for the outsider, those broken on the wheel of life, could not be denied, but as time passed his technique congealed into an awkward parody of his best theatrical productions. Next to Bergman, however, Sjöberg must be accounted the most significant Swedish director of that long, uneven period stretching from the departure of Sjöström and Stiller for Hollywood in the mid-1920's and the establishment of the Swedish Film Institute in 1963. *The Road to Heaven, Frenzy, Only a Mother* and *Miss Julie* are sufficient witness to his stature.

Bergman achieves world status

The final episode in an otherwise mediocre film, *Waiting Women* ("Kvinnors väntan", 1952) had revealed Bergman's delight in wry, sardonic comedy. *A Lesson in Love* ("En lektion i kärlek", 1954) strengthened this impression of a director for whom wit and repartee could act as an agreeable cloak for his melancholy, a trait he shares with such writers as Oscar Wilde and Somerset Maugham. By far his finest achievement in the genre of sophisticated comedy is *Smiles of a Summer Night* ("Sommarnattens leende", 1955), which signalled his arrival on the international scene as a film-maker of the foremost rank. The production won a major award at Cannes, and its success gave Berg-

Max von Sydow as the
Knight pitting his wits against
Death (Bengt Ekerot) in
The Seventh Seal.

Smiles of a Summer Night.
Gunnar Björnstrand,
Eva Dahlbeck and Jarl Kulle.

man—and Carl Anders Dymling at Svensk Filmindustri—the courage to proceed with *The Seventh Seal.*

Smiles of a Summer Night was by far the most complex film with which Bergman had been involved. The budget was high by Swedish standards (although probably less than $100,000 all told), shooting stretched over 55 days during a scorching summer in the south of the country, and to cap it all, Ulla Jacobsson, in one of the leading roles, was pregnant. But Bergman marshalled his forces with unerring skill, manoeuvring the nine principal characters as though they were figures in some 18th century dance, intermingling, joining hands, swinging from partner to partner with cheerful abandon while retaining an outward show of decorum. Set for the most part on a luxurious country estate, the film mocks all those who suffer from love's temptations and illusions. Age is represented by Madame Armfeldt, regal of bearing whether seated in bed or at the dining-table, and youth by the bashful Henrik, whose sneaking love for his father's fresh young wife finally gets the better of him. While most of the participants in this long summer night's dalliance are forced to cling to social niceties, Frid, the groom, and Petra, a visiting chambermaid, indulge their lusts in the open spaces of the park, free from the constricting decor of the mansion's many rococo rooms.

Nothing, however, could detract from the genuine feeling of Eva Dahlbeck's performance as Desirée, the actress who seeks her rewards in this world, rather than salvation in the next, and who hovers tantalisingly beyond the pompous grasp of Gunnar Björnstrand's Fredrik Egerman. Björnstrand's makeup, with hair cropped short at the brow, and a beard and moustache trimmed to leave a heart of flesh about his tight-lipped mouth, forms the most provocative of the "masks" that Bergman had used up to that point. Death, in *The Seventh Seal,* and Vogler, in *The Face,* must move among men with even more disturbing disguises.

In 1956 Bergman embarked on the film that has introduced his genius to successive generations of film students: *The Seventh Seal* ("Det sjunde inseglet"). Bergman's claim that it was intended as an allegory on the Cold War has long been made irrelevant by the abiding power of the work at a basic level of human emotion and characterisation. Who cannot side with the Knight in the magnificent folly of his duel with Death, pitting his skill at chess against an implacable force, searching the while for some worthwhile gesture to perform before submitting to his adversary? Max von Sydow, still in his mid-twenties when he played the role of the Knight, brings to the role a beguiling blend of detachment and instinctual passion that might be equalled only by Alec Guinness in his prime. For the first time, audiences outside Sweden recognised the brilliance of Bergman's regular team. Gunnar Fischer's photography had produced admirable results in films like *Summer Interlude* and *Smiles of a Summer Night,* but now foreign critics began to accord him his due. The contributions of Erik Nordgren, with his ominous musical accompaniment to *The Seventh Seal,* and P.A. Lundgren, the production designer whose recreation of medieval Sweden excelled the opulent costume epics of Hollywood, began to emerge more forcefully; while the ensemble quality of the performances was without parallel even in Europe. Most of the players were already appearing under Bergman's direction at Malmö City Theatre, and some with minor parts in *The Seventh Seal* and *Wild Strawberries*—among them Gunnel Lindblom, Åke Fridell, and Inga Landgré—had dominated the stage in a major capacity.

The Seventh Seal has survived by virtue not so much of startling technique as of a vivid approach to man's fundamental dilemmas. The film's sympathies oscillate between the Knight, orthodox in his devotion, human in his craving for a sign of God's presence, and his Squire, captious and cynical, yet reaching for a nip of schnapps to quell his fear of the Plague. The idealised figure of Bibi Andersson's Mia, who takes a fancy to the Knight and offers him some temporary respite from his anxieties, fits neatly into this landscape of the morality play and the comedian Nils Poppe, whose own forces had earned him a considerable reputation in Swedish cinema after the war, found himself at home in the role of Jof, part fool, part visionary.

Victor Sjöström, who had left his post as artistic adviser to Svensk

Victor Sjöström was lured back to the screen in 1957 by Ingmar Bergman to play opposite Bibi Andersson in *Wild Strawberries*.

Filmindustri at the end of the 1940's, was successfully persuaded by Bergman to take the lead in *Wild Strawberries* ("Smultronstället", 1957), the story of an aging professor forced to revisit certain crucial sectors of his own egocentric life. Sjöström had encouraged Bergman in earlier days, and the two men held each other in high esteem. Without this magnificent central performance—incarnation might be a better word—*Wild Strawberries* would be considerably diminished. Its technique has not worn so well as that of some Bergman films of the 1950's, and its image of the younger generation remains facile and unconvincing. But the film still has enormous presence. The opening nightmare is achieved with startling simplicity and imagination, and the wave of human emotion that eventually invades the icy indifference of so many of the characters gave the lie to Bergman's already established reputation for Nordic pessimism. Like all Bergman's great works of his middle period, *Wild Strawberries* involves its protagonist in a journey of crucial significance. Victor Sjöström's professor travels physically southwards, to Lund, where he is to receive an honorary doctorate, but psychologically reaches back through time on a voyage of expiation. Loneliness, and the fear of loneliness, assails many Bergman characters; in *Wild Strawberries,* its source is revealed unmistakably as self-conceit.

Curiously, for all his love of Strindberg, Bergman did not attempt to bring his plays to the screen. Sjöberg's *Miss Julie* had proved that Strindberg's narrow, if piercing, vision could be expanded to fill the more open spaces of the cinema, and so too did Anders Henrikson's version of two Strindberg short stories, under the title *Married* ("Giftas", 1956). The fine calibre of Swedish acting was evident in the performances by Anita Björk as a glacial, frustrated young woman who fears the male sex, and by Gunnel Broström, as a stiff and masculine schoolmistress who promulgates the intellectual precepts associated with Ibsen's heroines.

Bergman's interest in the female condition emerged more powerfully still in *So Close to Life* or *Brink of Life,* as it is also known ("Nära livet", 1958) which was set in a maternity ward. Three women are under the microscope: one has just suffered a miscarriage, another appears healthy and cheerful, but is overdue in giving birth, and the third is pregnant with an illegitimate child. The intensity of the dialogue combines with the clinical environment of the hospital to create a work of severe tension and vigour.

Altogether more intriguing, and closer to Bergman's heart, was *The Face,* also known as *The Magician* ("Ansiktet", 1958), which starred Max von Sydow, the director's favourite actor of the Malmö period, as a reluctant charlatan, laden with the pompous name of Albert Emanuel Vogler, detained in a Stockholm house and taunted by a haughty doctor who lays siege to his adversary's elusive attributes. During his several years as a stage producer, Bergman had come to regard his audience with mingled gratitude and loathing. *The Face* lays bare these feelings, pitting the entertainer, complete with mumbo jumbo and fake assistants, against the rational cool of the scientist, who longs to perform a post-mortem on Vogler in an effort to explain the artist's influence.

The visualisation of this conflict is inspired, even by Bergman's standards. Striking a chord that uncannily blends chuckles and suspense, Bergman brings his Gothic shadow-play to a climax in a cluttered attic, where Vogler deceives his opponent and reduces him to a whimpering idiot, before exposing himself to his "public" without his false wig and beard, and riding off to the Royal Palace to perform for the King. In most respects, *The Face* is a splendid exercise in expressionistic pastiche, but although one may laugh at the gullibility of the characters and the crudeness of the special effects laid on by Vogler and his troupe, there remains the disturbing sense of a director who has one firmly in his grasp, and who repeatedly turns the joke to his own advantage.

The Face opened in Stockholm at Christmas, 1958, just one week after Bergman had staged his final production at Malmö City Theatre. His life was at a watershed both on a personal and professional level. A more economical, ascetic style can be traced in his films from around this time. *The Virgin Spring* ("Jungfrukällan", 1960) contained some of his Malmö faithfuls, among them Max von Sydow, Gunnel Lindblom, and Gudrun Brost. But new talents, such as Allan Edwall, emerged also, and the film marked the arrival in Bergman's camp of Sven Ny-

Moment of Truth; Karin is confronted by one of the beggars in *The Virgin Spring*.

kvist, a cameraman who had worked on numerous scenes in *Sawdust and Tinsel,* and who would henceforth be companion to Bergman on all his films. Gunnar Fischer, whose luminous, crystalline lighting and camerawork had graced the masterpieces of the 1950's, was now rejected by Bergman. Both these great cinematographers have served Swedish cinema well, and just as Fischer's technique would not have suited Bergman's visual style of the 1960's and beyond, so Nykvist's might have been incongruous in the more baroque and brooding Bergman films of the two earlier decades.

The Virgin Spring signifies this crossroads in Bergman's work and life

Sven Nykvist first joined Ingmar Bergman in the late 1950's to film *The Virgin Spring*.

more sharply than any other film. It is the last screen work in which he genuflects to the religious authority of his upbringing, and in which God possesses the dimensions of traditional dogma. It also marks Bergman's final salute to the medieval order. "During the 1950's," he has since conceded, "I needed a severe and schematic conception of the world to get away from the formless, vague and the obscure, in which I was stuck. So I turned to the dogmatic Christianity of the Middle Ages with its clear dividing lines between Good and Evil. Later I felt tied by it, I felt as though I were imprisoned."

Filmed in a vigorous, turbulent manner reminiscent of Akira Kurosawa's Japanese epics, *The Virgin Spring* hinges on pride and guilt. Pride proves the downfall of the young virgin, Karin, and guilt disfigures the majestic mien of her father, Töre, who must bear the agony of discovering that his daughter has been raped and killed by three vagabonds in the forest. Like many Bergman films, this smacks of ritual, and the inner tension may be traced to the struggle between paganism and Christianity, between the primeval forces of Thor and Odin, and the more forgiving, more hypocritical religion of the modern era.

For Bergman, as for Swedish cinema in toto, the 1950's ended on a note of failure. *The Devil's Eye* ("Djävulens öga", 1960) was an obstinately portentous comedy about a resurrected Don Juan, sent up to earth from the nether regions by a Satan who believes that the stye in his eye is caused by the existence of a virgin—Bibi Andersson, no less. The music of Domenico Scarlatti, played on the harpsichord by Käbi Laretei, afforded one of the film's few genuine pleasures. "I detest the idea that some of my films, especially the bad ones, are going to survive," declared Bergman after this fiasco.

Other gifted directors
Even if Swedish film production in the 1950's and early 1960's was dominated by two masters, Bergman and Sjöberg, other directors were creating films which attracted attention.

Sweden has often served as a sanctuary for political and artistic refugees. Chief among them at the close of the 1950's was the Austrian, Peter Weiss (later celebrated for his *Marat-Sade*), who revived the ideals of the surrealist avant-garde with *Mirage* ("Hägringen", 1959), a haunting, hallucinatory skein of images involving a young man approaching a great city—the outsider confronted with the sexual and social contradictions of modern Sweden.

One Summer of Happiness, Arne Mattsson's film from 1951 which caused some controversy.

Arne Mattsson

In 1951 Arne Mattsson's *One Summer of Happiness* ("Hon dansade en sommar") caused some controversy. The harbinger of such later Swedish sex films as *I am Curious Yellow* and *As the Naked Wind from the Sea* ("...som havets nakna vind", 1968), this production contained just a few moments of titillating exposure (the young lovers embracing in some reeds near a lakeshore, for instance) and rehearsed the traditional Scandinavian clash between reproof and indulgence, with two young people struggling to express their desires in the face of a small community's distaste.

The film, quaint and often gratuitous, did have the merit of introducing the talent of Ulla Jacobsson, who later starred in Bergman's *Smiles of a Summer Night.* Nor was there any doubt as to Mattsson's ability to set a scene and then build up its emotional tension with bold, stabbing montage. Ironically, his subsequent films, *The Bread of Love* ("Kärlekens bröd", 1953), *Salka Valka* (1954), and *The People of Hemsö* ("Hemsöborna", 1955) are all superior to *One Summer of Happiness,* but their subject matter was too closely involved with Nordic society for them to excite any real following abroad. *Salka Valka,* based on a novel by the Icelandic Nobel prizewinner, Halldór Laxness, established the mood and tang of a fishing village, and inspired the finest performance of her career from Gunnel Broström; while *The Bread of Love* turned eastwards to the Russian-Finnish Winter War of 1939–40. Mattsson's tracking shots in this latter production glide over the snow again and again until they acquire a kind of mesmeric, incantory significance, as in the films of Alain Resnais. Man is absorbed by the elements. His mind as well as his body is pierced by the relentless cold. Much the same could be said of *The People of Hemsö,* the most gripping of the various screen versions of August Strindberg's novel about a tight-knit community in the Stockholm skerries, which ends with the main character's being dragged down beneath the ice by the weight of his wife's funeral casket.

In later years Mattsson succumbed to the allure of easy commercial subjects, and produced no further work of lasting interest.

Arne Sucksdorff

As respite from the gloom of Bergman's output, and the academic formalism of Sjöberg's, there came like a broad ray of sunlight the unpretentious masterpiece by Arne Sucksdorff, *The Great Adventure* ("Det stora äventyret", 1953). Two boys, growing up on a farm in central Sweden, capture an otter, and during the winter months they tame her. When spring comes, they make the mistake of turning their heads as the otter is dipped in the lake and all at once she has vanished, setting out on her own "great adventure". Sucksdorff's craftsmanship is excelled only by his unerring alertness to the changing seasons, to those subtle inflections of nature that mark the arrival of a predator or victim. "In *The Great Adventure*," Sucksdorff has said, "I try to show a acceptance of life and other human beings. After all, one of the main human rights is the right to make mistakes!" (referring to Anders' resentment towards his younger brother for divulging the secret of the otter to their parents).

This was followed by a documentary evocation of a remote tribe in India—*The Flute and the Arrow* ("En djungelsaga", 1957) which was memorable for its 'scope imagery. However, by the beginning of the 1960's Arne Sucksdorff ran out of creative inspiration and his fictional film about some marauding youths in the Swedish countryside, *The Boy in the Tree* ("Pojken i trädet", 1961) lacked conviction. At least his swansong, *My Home Is Copacabana,* set in the slums of Rio de Janeiro, would salvage some significant part of Sucksdorff's prestige as an observer of children in natural surroundings.

The Great Adventure.

A New Era, 1962–1970

The Swedish cinema was on its knees in the early 1960's. The industry depended heavily on American imports and on its own "studio" productions from Svensk Filmindustri, Sandrews, and Europa Film. Bergman continued to forge ahead along his particular stony path, enhancing the early years of the decade with his remarkable trilogy, *Through a Glass Darkly, Winter Light,* and *The Silence.* Alf Sjöberg, on the other hand, suffered a serious reverse with *The Judge* ("Domaren") in 1960, and Carl Anders Dymling, for so long the enlightened head of Svensk Filmindustri, died in 1961.

A combination of declining audiences, due in the main to the impact of television (which had come to Sweden in 1956), and a punitive entertainments tax, had dissuaded the independent producer from embarking on any enterprise that smacked of experiment or social comment. Nor was there a film school at which neophyte directors or technicians could be trained.

The irony of all this is that, in spite of the Herculean effort that was made to overcome the prevailing difficulties, the identical situation has recurred in the early 1980's, except that the inroads made by the video boom have replaced the threat from television—which in some quarters is even looked upon as the saviour of the cinema!

The creation of the Film Institute

Two influential booklets appeared in 1962. One was a diatribe against the quality of Swedish film, *The Vision in the Swedish Cinema* ("Visionen i svensk film"), written by Bo Widerberg the writer and director, who argued that films made in Sweden were divorced from real life, and tended towards escapism and character stereotypes. Widerberg also attacked Ingmar Bergman, the high priest of the Swedish cinema during

Bo Widerberg.

the previous decade: "Bergman welcomes the coarsest myths about us and ours, emphasises the false notions which foreigners love to have confirmed," he wrote, going on to reproach the master for his "vertical cinema" in which man is either humbled or exalted. "The book was a protest," declared Widerberg with the hindsight of after years. "Every new Swedish film was a disaster; it had absolutely no connection with modern society."

The other key publication was *Can We Afford Culture?* ("Har vi råd med kultur?") by Harry Schein. Schein had fled from Austria to Sweden during the war, had taught himself Swedish in his teens, made a sparkling career in chemical engineering, and delighted readers of the arch-intellectual magazine, "BLM" ("Bonniers Litterära Magasin") with his film criticism. Now, with friends in high places, he used his influence to strike a mortal blow at the entertainments tax, which he perceived as being at the root of the difficulties undermining Swedish cinema. His plan of action, as advocated in *Can We Afford Culture?*, involved the abandonment of the 25% entertainments tax, and its replacement by a levy of 10% on each cinema ticket sold, the proceeds of which would be funnelled into a new organ altogether—the Swedish Film Institute.

This income would be divided heavily in favour of quality production. Some 30% was to be distributed to all Swedish films in direct proportion to their box-office receipts, while a further 33% was allotted to quality awards to Swedish features (decided by a panel of "experts"). The remaining 37% was to be divided between costs for administration, archives, public relations, film clubs and awards for short films. Schein liked this system because it ensured that only the final result counted in establishing a production's merit. "The Swedish Film Institute expresses in this way," he maintained, "the status of a free film production in a modern welfare state, in which the government abstains from direct control of production, economically, thematically, or artistically, provided that the film industry recognises its responsibility not only towards its shareholders but towards the art of film as well."

(Ten years later Schein would have to eat his words, and the role of the Institute changed direction, supporting virtually all projects from their inception and reducing the amount of cash available for quality awards.)

The Institute did not finally open its doors until July 1, 1963, and when it did, its watchword was quality. In his book, Schein had written, "The case of Ingmar Bergman—and the general development in the international film market—has taught the Swedish film industry a lesson. Its chance to survive in the harsh international climate is to invest in quality films." Although this was a principle already championed by Charles Magnusson during the silent era, it is questionable if production houses in Sweden in the early 1960's really wanted to invest in quality. Anders Sandrew had died in 1957, and in 1961 the untimely death of Carl Anders Dymling was a severe blow. So the giants of the Swedish film world shifted forward with caution, suspicious of Schein and his motives.

However, stung by Schein's criticism, and startled by the sheer number of young directors brandishing screenplays, the industry somehow contrived to offer youth an opportunity. Of the 177 features made after the setting up of the Film Institute, and up to the end of 1969, no fewer than 50 were signed by first-time directors. One must go to France at the end of the 1950's to find any kind of parallel with this flowering. Given the development of world cinema over the past twenty years, it is inconceivable that it could be repeated.

Pioneers of the Sixties

Three man led the charge into the new era. Bo Widerberg himself, whose *The Baby Carriage* was made before the foundation of the Institute; Vilgot Sjöman, with *The Mistress* and *491;* and the Finnish-born Jörn Donner, with *A Sunday in September.* These individuals had certain things in common. They had all written about the art of the film. Sjöman had even been to Hollywood for a year of studying the industry. Donner had helped found the Finnish Film Archive, and had served a term as film critic of Sweden's largest morning newspaper, "Dagens Nyheter". Widerberg, like Schein, had published articles on film in "BLM".

All of them came from a literary background, and the act of writing a screenplay therefore seemed a natural precondition for the budding director. They were further united by a concern for the fate of human relationships in a materialistic world, and looked with a degree of scepticism on the smooth, somewhat complacent façade of Swedish welfare policy. They sought out the fate of the individual in a country that taught its citizens to think above all of the community. Finally, they were all over 30 years of age when their first feature appeared, so that the myth of a "movie brats" generation in 1963 is false. But of course by comparison with Sjöberg, Sucksdorff, and Mattsson, they *were* rather young—and even younger in ideas than in years.

Numerous other directors followed them on to the scene—and almost immediately into the international arena, for festivals soon began to invite the work of the new Swedish film-makers, and individual triumphs (such as Widerberg's *Elvira Madigan* and Sjöman's *I Am Curious—Yellow*) brought talk of Swedish cinema into even the most conservative of drawing-room conversations. Talent took on many guises. Mai Zetterling was an actress who brought to the cinema a passionate belief in women's rights. Jan Troell was the most brilliantly endowed cinematographer of his generation, and would re-create the visual glories of the silent era. Johan Bergenstråhle regarded cinema as a medium through which to criticise the failings of Swedish society past and present. Jan Halldoff echoed the dream-wishes and escapades of young adults reared on the pop music revolution of the Beatles. Jonas Cornell conceived of film as theorem, with sequences ingeniously plotted in dialectic relation to one another while still retaining the traditional narrative form.

Cornell, in fact, was probably the most distinguished graduate of the Swedish Film Institute's Film School, where the Principal was Rune Waldekranz, a producer and scholar (not so uncommon a combination in Sweden as in other countries!). Unfortunately, the identity of the Film School faded during the 1970's, when its activities were absorbed into the Institute of the Dramatic Arts. It is arguable that only in a first-class film school do enthusiasts learn the value of a career not just in direction, but also in producing, editing, design, or screenwriting.

Freedom of expression: love and sex in the Sixties
The quality awards bestowed by the Institute on films irrespective of their public success allowed film-makers to relax when tackling their creative dilemmas. They also enjoyed the luxury of freedom of speech

where politics was concerned, and freedom of expression where sex was involved. Foreign audiences were lured to Swedish films—even to so stark a production as Bergman's *The Silence*—by the whiff of salaciousness, and deterred by the Swedish penchant for social argument. In *I Am Curious—Yellow* the two themes ran parallel to each other, and resulted in large attendances but precious few converts to the cause of Vilgot Sjöman's social and erotic anarchy.

Love, surfaced in many forms in the Swedish cinema of the 1960's. Most appealing to Swedish audiences was *Dear John* ("Käre John", 1964), directed by Lars-Magnus Lindgren from a novel by Olle Länsberg. Jarl Kulle, as the cargo vessel skipper, and Christina Schollin, as the wayward vulnerable Anita, seemed to embody everyone's ideal of the intimate couple. Each has been bruised by life, yet each believes in passion and the happy ending.

Bo Widerberg

Sex in Swedish cinema is handled with most tenderness and natural awe by Bo Widerberg. His characters experience physical love with an intensity and distinctness that elude most of Widerberg's Scandinavian contemporaries. There is nothing cruel or lascivious in films like *The Baby Carriage, Love 65,* or *Elvira Madigan;* nor is there a degree of romanticism so acute as to obliterate the panic of guilt and the thrill of emotional loss.

Widerberg left school early and took a variety of jobs, including a post in a mental hospital and a night editorship on a small provincial newspaper in southern Sweden. During the late 1950's, he acquired a modest reputation as a novelist, and in 1961 made a short film for TV called *The Boy and the Kite* ("Pojken och draken", 1961), in collaboration with Jan Troell. In his feature films he set out to communicate his passionate beliefs to a wider audience, to come to grips with the problems confronting a modern democratic society. "I do not make films just to show how Sweden looks today," he announced, "but since I want the people I am portraying to act against a living background, it follows automatically that Sweden, this experiment in welfare, forms this background." Yet Widerberg would reject the work of Jean-Luc Godard as being too cerebral, and fall beneath the spell of two more spontaneous directors, François Truffaut and John Cassavetes. He went to considerable lengths to secure a feeling of immediacy in his conversation scenes. *Elvira Madigan* was based on a 25-page script without dialogue. Widerberg told Thommy Berggren and Pia Degermark their lines about 3 minutes prior to shooting.

The role of women in the contemporary world marks the films of the early 1960's in Sweden. In Widerberg's *The Baby Carriage/The Pram* ("Barnvagnen", 1962), a young girl, Britt (played by Inger Taube), becomes pregnant by a rock singer, moves into his apartment, but finds herself too immature to cope with the responsibilities of a husband. She hankers after more intellectual stimulus, finding it in the shape of the shy and kindly Björn. But Björn is in turn dominated by his mother, and the budding relationship withers. Britt refuses to bow to traditional expectations of feminine behaviour, however, and in the final shots Widerberg shows her wheeling her perambulator through the streets, a face in the crowd, a grown-up woman making independent decisions.

Like Mai Zetterling and Vilgot Sjöman (see below), Widerberg was attracted by the taboos that lay beneath the surface of Sweden's materially comfortable life in the 1960's.

Taboos seep to the surface in various Swedish films of the mid- and late 1960's. Widerberg, in *Love 65* ("Kärlek 65") again assumes an autobiographical stance, even choosing a leading actor (Keve Hjelm) who resembled him and whose role as a film director shuffling between wife and mistress mirrored the uncertainty of the artist when confronted with the swiftly-changing moral landscape of the decade. Like Fellini's $8^1/_2$, this fragment of autobiographical testament by Bo Widerberg contains declarations of intent and yearning. "I should like to be more simple without lying," says Keve. "I should like to make a film that was as real and as concrete as something you say across a breakfast table." And later: "What has happened to the cinema is that it has gone and got itself a morality. It has finally got enough courage to say that it is only film. Nothing else. Godard says that a film is the truth 24 times a

Thommy Berggren and Pia Degermark in *Elvira Madigan*.

second. He can't bind himself further. And for Antonioni the choice of every camera angle is a question of ethics. You can no longer make two-hour films with a beginning, a middle, and an end. The old type of film was a lie even in its basic form. It made a claim of continuity. Unbrokenness. It told of a world that was whole and unbroken and that could be grasped in only one way."

Brave words. But Widerberg himself discovered that to engage an audience one must offer it signposts along the way. Film is not some kind of advanced orienteering. *Love 65* proved a flop, while *Elvira*

71

Madigan (1967), which traced an exquisitely simple storyline, brought Widerberg ringing acclaim around the world. The dramatic catalyst is the oldest in civilisation's book: the clandestine affair, linking a Swedish Count and a girl from a circus milieu in a desperate, intoxicating passion that leads them to commit suicide together.

Widerberg's longing is for a society that will accommodate such deviations of the heart. "Perhaps the time will come when one can choose more than a single life," says Count Sixten to his Elvira. He refuses to acknowledge the social pressures on him to return to his wife, his children, and his regiment. He can see nothing beyond the blade of grass directly before his eyes. "But without grass," he tells his friend from the army, "the world would be nothing."

Sex and violence are absent from *Elvira Madigan.* Even the moment when Sixten pulls the trigger to shoot his love is transformed by Widerberg into a lasting image of aching beauty, the sound of the gun off-screen freezing Elvira into immobility, at the split-second she releases from her hands a butterfly, that elusive symbol of serendipity. The film allows nature and the elements to point the tale forward. The food of the earth, and water: Sixten and Elvira catch fish and devour their raspberries and cream. The portents of winter: rain that exiles Sixten from the room where Elvira is present, the wind that scours trees and bushes as the couple pass through the woods for their final breakfast. And the metaphors for death: a bottle of wine that spills and gurgles out its blood-red contents on a snow-white cloth, the talk of bayonets slicing through to the body's musculature.

Mozart's 21st Piano Concerto, and Vivaldi's Violin Concerti, are matched to this sunstruck tragedy as though by some magic alchemy. True, Widerberg labours the Mozart theme, but with *Elvira Madigan* he demonstrates without question his supreme gift for lyrical cinema, his sensual affection for natural light an objects. It was no coincidence that in the same year another saga of doomed outsiders, *Bonnie and Clyde,* entranced audiences in many countries. In Sweden it was perhaps ironic that a society so dedicated to the good of the community as a whole should have embraced a work of art so resolutely on the side of the individual—even an individual who, as Widerberg discreetly emphasised, could not relate to those beyond his own social class.

Jörn Donner

In his film *A Sunday in September* ("En söndag i september", 1963) Jörn Donner cast his cool eye at the hypocrisy of the wedding in white—with the bride already pregnant and love flying out of the window. Marriage affords Birgitta and Stig an opportunity to escape the clutches of their bourgeois families—but it also clasps them in a steadily tightening vice of egotism and misunderstanding. Stig, like most men, can find some meaning in his everyday work, but for Birgitta there is no channel of expression. Donner, by comparison with Widerberg, is pessimistic about the prospects for marital emancipation. His couple decides on a divorce, and tackles it with the dispassionate gravity accorded a business transaction. Donner attempts to link the instability and despair of his characters to Swedish society of the period, even beginning *A Sunday in September* with some brief street interviews in which passers-by are asked about the possibilities open to love in the contemporary world.

The following year, Donner made *To Love* ("Att älska"), which sought to revive the mordant, sophisticated comedy style of Mauritz Stiller and to comment on the antic dance of modern sexual relationships. The film starred Harriet Andersson and the late Zbigniew Cybulski, who had come to prominence in the films of Andrzej Wajda in Poland. Donner's other Swedish films were more earnest and less successful, although he would renew his career in his native Finland during the late Sixties. He returned to Sweden as Managing Director of the Swedish Film Institute in 1978, resigning in 1981.

Vilgot Sjöman

Sjöman's *The Mistress* ("Älskarinnan", 1962) also dealt with the pressures opposing a woman's emancipation in the Sweden of the 1960's. Bibi Andersson, bearing no name in the film, finds herself caught between the desires of a married man (Max von Sydow) and a more

Vilgot Sjöman.

regular boyfriend (Per Myrberg). The plot of *The Mistress* is as hackneyed as its title; even the conclusion, in which Bibi Andersson turns her back on both men and resolves to start afresh, is hardly an original solution to the dilemma. Observers were impressed, however, by Sjöman's use of the wide-screen scope format, by the rigour of his exposition, and by his rejection of such traditional props as a music score. The bulk of the film is devoted to a single day in the girl's apartment. Her lover telephones to say that he can take her out. She promptly cancels her date with her boyfriend and waits eagerly. Then, in one telephone call after another, the lover delays their meeting. She begins to realise how precarious and distracting the management of two men can be.

Sjöman imposed himself on the Swedish cinema with his observation and his grasp of feminine psychology, gifts that manifested themselves in *The Dress* ("Klänningen", 1964) but that sank amid a tide of self-pity, thinly-veiled disgust, and a consuming sense of guilt, as a widow and her daughter fall in love with the same man—a variation on the plot of *The Mistress*, although the source of the film was a novel by Ulla Isaksson, author of Bergman's *The Virgin Spring*.

Clandestine feelings lie at the base of most of Sjöman's films; their revelation is equated with both freedom and turmoil. In *My Sister My Love* ("Syskonbädd 1782", 1966), the taboo of incest is presented in the stylised context of an 18th century in which frightening demarcation lines were drawn between the classes and where a *fin-de-siècle* lassitude led to perversion and the triumph of the senses over reason. "The

Bibi Andersson in
The Mistress.

Church had little power and people sought emancipation and rationalism," says Sjöman. "But for all that, people in the period knew what it was to give way to dark and subconscious impulses." Some years before Sjöman wrote his screenplay, a brother and sister in Gävle (in northern Sweden) conceived a child together and were separated by the law. Sjöman re-creates the past in order to comment on the present, and does so with leering relish.

Sjöman's next film brought him into headlong conflict with the censors of the day. *I Am Curious—Yellow* ("Jag är nyfiken—gul", 1967) was only the first half of a massive four-hour investigation into the moral and social state of Sweden in the mid-1960's. The president of the State Censorship Board felt that the film should not be released without cuts. But, after prolonged debate, his opinion was overruled and *I Am Curious—Yellow* proved an enormous public success. Abroad, Sjöman's audacity was greeted with cold stares by many authorities—most notably the US customs, who impounded the film until the gathering momentum of intellectual fury (Norman Mailer was among several who signed protests in favour of the Swedish director) forced them to release the picture. It soon became one of the most popular foreign films of the decade in the ᵁnited States, and Grove Press published both the screenplays of the *Yellow* and *Blue* "editions" as well as a book of reminiscences about the production by Sjöman, entitled *I Was Curious.*

Lena Nyman, playing a young girl of her own generation, is the ubiquitous heroine of *I Am Curious.* Seeking by interviews and research to ascertain if Sweden has changed, politically and socially, during the thirty years of Social Democrat rule, she finds that her own personality crumbles under the pressures of private life. Her father is bitter and maudlin by turns; her boyfriend lets her down. Finally, this lively blonde girl recognises that she cannot cling to her ideal of non-violence, and that it is inapplicable to both private and public life.

Sjöman's style is born of *cinéma-vérité,* and really does give the impression of a filmed *experience,* in which Sjöman is as much involved as anyone as he watches Lena's love affairs with a jealous eye. In the *Blue* edition, he describes Lena's brief but harrowing encounter with a singer

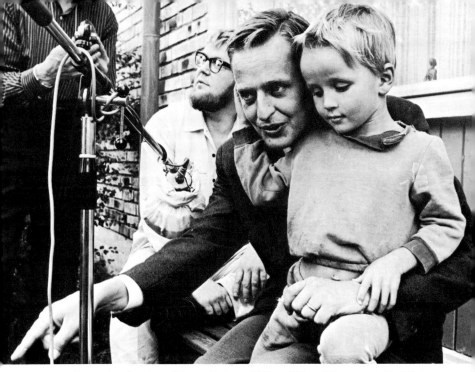

From the shooting of *I am Curious—Yellow*. Vilgot Sjöman and Olof Palme (then Minister of Education).

in southern Sweden, a woman who turns out to have lesbian tendencies and rejects Lena. At the close of this latter-day odyssey, Lena rides her bicycle in the opposite direction to a students' protest march.

Mai Zetterling

Sex as violence. Sex as perversion. Sex as humiliation. This connotation could be found not just in the work of Vilgot Sjöman, but also in films like the Danish director, Henning Carlsen's *The Cats* ("Kattorna", 1965) and Mai Zetterling's *Loving Couples* ("Älskande par", 1964) and *Night Games* ("Nattlek", 1966). *The Cats* derived from a mediocre

Loving Couples. Jan Malmsjö, Frank Sundström and Eva Dahlbeck.

stage play by Walentin Chorell about the tensions among women working in a laundry, but *Loving Couples* boasted an impeccable pedigree, based as it was on Agnes von Krusenstjerna's suite of novels, *The Misses von Pahlen,* published between 1930 and 1935 and evoking the era of the First World War in Sweden.

Nostalgia soon succumbs to feminist anger. Men are to blame for the misfortunes and aberrations described in *Loving Couples* (even the title is ironic). The healthy Angela comments, "Marriage—it's like falling asleep for the rest of your life," and the barren Adèle bursts out at the wedding feast, "There isn't any love—it's just beds, dirt and slime!" The men are divided into those who grasp their sexual gratification without a thought for the consequences, and those who, in the words of one elder of the von Pahlen family, stay at home "lapping cream like castrated tomcats." Ms. Zetterling manages to communicate this vitriolic message with an admirable clarity of word and image. The memories of the various characters are dovetailed into one another with unostentatious fluidity, while the soundtrack is intelligent from the opening moments, as the squeaking of hospital trolleys sets the right tone of friction and anguish in an outwardly ordered society. The family doctor lets fall some of the tarter observations: "We're a wise family, Vicar," he says, "We don't hold with feelings, they're too vulgar."

The tang of Luis Buñuel, even of Bergman, that one detected in *Loving Couples*—which was, after all, Mai Zetterling's first feature for the cinema—disappeared in *Night Games*, with its altogether more cruel and decadent mood. Jan, the protagonist, tries to achieve re-birth by tracing the life and experiences of his childhood self. Past and present are blended subtly and without pause, as in Sjöberg's *Miss Julie*, but by the second half of the film the divertissements at the manor where Jan's "mother" holds sway have assumed too dominant a role. "I tried to film a story of modern Europe," claimed Mai Zetterling. "I try to be honest, so it shows signs of decadence. Perverted sex is one of these signs, perhaps the most dramatically obvious, and I use it because I believe you can only come to a positive view of things by passing through innumerable negative views." The only solution open to Jan is to destroy this house of sin, and the consummate decisiveness of the conclusion is perhaps the best moment in the film. Guests snatch what loot they can from the doomed area. The fire that reduces the manor to ruins may also purify Jan's soul. Yet without the orgies there would not be much left of *Night Games*. The very evils that the director attacks provide the ballast for her own film.

The porn syndrome

Films like *Dear John* and its predecessor, Lindgren's *Do You Believe in Angels?* ("Änglar, finns dom?", 1961), emerged in a bizarre symbiosis with a stream of films on the mechanics of sexual relationships. Among the best of these exploitation movies was *I—a Woman* ("Jag—en kvinna", 1965), featuring Essy Persson as an innocent young nurse whose intercourse with a hospital patient opens a vivid world of lust and its techniques. Among the worst was *The Language of Love* ("Kärlekens språk", 1969), a kind of staged documentary on the numerous positions and erogenous zones that provoke sexual satisfaction. The film was "bad" not because of its full frontal frankness where sex was concerned (stirring up protracted court hearings in the United States and a demonstration by 30,000 people in London's Trafalgar Square against Swedish "porn, suicide, alcoholism, and gonorrhea"), but simply because its modest level of competence and lack of inspiration robbed it of feeling and genuine eroticism. *The Language of Love* was made for 700,000 kronor, and brought in more than 6.5 million kronor in its first full season of release. Not surprisingly, such an economic miracle spawned a series of cloned imitations, all of which furthered Sweden's reputation for mechanised, unemotional sexual habits.

One man's fate

The Sixties was coloured by a mood of inquiry, as *I Am Curious* showed. Much of this investigative reporting dealt with political and social issues, but two of the period's most significant and enjoyable films gazed at life through artistic and emotional eyes. Both Widerberg's *Raven's End* ("Kvarteret korpen", 1963) and Jan Troell's *Here Is Your Life* ("Här har du ditt liv", 1966) returned to the past. They pound with rebellion against the conventional fate of poverty and drunkenness; their young heroes refuse to be swept like stray logs down the heedless current of the years.

Raven's End, set in Malmö in 1936, paints a stark picture of working-class life. Anders' father is a failed underwear salesman; his mother scrubs and washes to bolster the family income. They are three months behind with the rent. Anders, however, nurses the dream of becoming a novelist, and even though his first manuscript is rejected, he plucks up courage to quit his miserable tenement environment. Frustration throbs beneath every scene. "If you shout loud enough someone's bound to hear you, but they're too far away to understand what you're saying," reflects Anders. In the train to see a potential publisher in Stockholm, he

Keve Hjelm and Thommy Berggren in a scene from *Raven's End*.

stares out of the window and explains offscreen how not even a thermom-
eter may be had in his apartment block, and a neighbour's boy lies
seriously ill as a consequence.

The implication of Widerberg's ending to the film is that Anders has
abandoned Raven's End, preferring to pursue his literary vocation rather than to cope with the social injustices of his background and to
improve them by on-the-spot efforts. For Anders, the pen is mightier
than the welfare system and the selfishness of Widerberg's alter ego is
compounded by his leaving behind in Malmö a pregnant girlfriend.

Like Anders, the central personality of *Here Is Your Life* is a nomad,
trudging from district to district and job to job as he comes to terms

with the hazards of life in the Sweden of 1914 to 1918. Olof is the creation of Eyvind Johnson, whose tetralogy *The Novels about Olof* mirrored his own youth in Norrbotten. The boy (marvellously played by Eddie Axberg) finds himself confronted with laughter and death, poverty and avarice, and the first stirrings of sexual desire. He works in such diverse settings as a sawmill and a local cinema. He makes friends with a young anarchist and through him becomes acquainted with the teaching of Karl Marx and the need for social change in Sweden. At the end we see him like a speck in the snow-packed forest road, marching south in search of his future.

Johnson's novels offered the perfect basis for such an epic film (almost three hours in length), but the flavour and texture of *Here Is Your Life* suggested that an exciting new talent had arrived on the Swedish scene. Jan Troell, a former schoolteacher in Malmö, shy, observant, and a magician with a camera, proved himself overnight to be the direct heir of Victor Sjöström. Once again, Swedish country life was celebrated with a visual poetry and a human understanding rare in the cinema of the 1960's, a time when urban crises formed the dominant theme. Troell was fortunate in teaming with Bengt Forslund, a young producer at Svensk Filmindustri who had also yearned to make a film of Johnson's novels and whose facility as a screenwriter helped Troell enunciate feelings and ideas that might otherwise have lain dormant in his tender imagery. Shot on location in the far north of Sweden during the summer, autumn, and winter of 1965, *Here Is Your Life* retrieved Swedish audiences with a rush, breaking all records at Stockholm's leading cinema, "Röda Kvarn", and even selling to several overseas territories—among them the United States, where it was released in a heavily abridged version.

If *Here Is Your Life* proclaims the Swedish qualities of phlegm, self-sufficiency, and gallows humour, noting in its characters a modest wisdom and an unspoken courage in the face of nature's capricious demands, then Troell's second feature film, *Who Saw Him Die?* ("Ole dole doff", 1968) casts a darker glance at Swedish traits. Painfully contemporary in hue, *Who Saw Him Die?* portrays the travails of a

Jan Troell during the shooting of his first American film, *Zandy's Bride*.

Here is Your Life. Stig Törnblom and Eddie Axberg

schoolteacher in Troell's home town of Malmö. In *Frenzy*, Bergman and Sjöberg had presented the pupil as victim, and the teacher as villain. Here, a quarter of a century later, the roles are reversed: the children in Mårtensson's class torment him physically and psychologically while he, undermined by a cold and childless marriage, proves ineffectual because he sides instinctively with the class against himself. In some respects, Mårtensson resembles a misunderstood pupil. When he appears before the principal to explain his slapping a boy in class, he accepts the inevitable rebuke as silently and evasively as though he were a child. On his free days, he stands like a wounded bird in the Malmö docks, watching the ships being loaded for far-off lands.

Once again, Troell's eye for the impressionist image sustains his work — birds trotting in isolation over the stones of the city streets in winter, dead fish staring upwards to reflect Mårtensson's misery, a dark tunnel of trees with a sunlit glade in the distance. A further revelation of Troell's sensitivity as a director emerges in the soundtrack, with its minutiae of effects — the slamming of desks, the cacophony of children's voices, the myriad background stirrings of a forest as Mårtensson chats with a sympathetic woman colleague.

Bergman's response to the spirit of the Sixties

Ingmar Bergman whittled away at his religious obsession in the three films of the early 1960's that marked a new phase in his development as an artist: *Through a Glass Darkly* ("Såsom i en spegel", 1961), *Winter Light* ("Nattvardsgästerna", 1963), and *The Silence* ("Tystnaden", 1963). Eventually, at the close of the final film, the presence of God has vanished altogether. A boy reads on a scrap of paper "some words in a foreign language" bequeathed him by his dying aunt. The journey to this end, which Bergman termed "a reduction", is long and painful, starting on a Baltic island where four members of a family lacerate one another's feelings and complexes like the quartet in *Long Day's Journey into Night*. David, a novelist, shoulders the greatest burden of guilt — he has put his career before his relatives (an offence committed also by Ingrid Bergman's concert pianist in *Autumn Sonata)* and when

84

his daughter topples into insanity, David is powerless to help her; he can but observe.

If *Through a Glass Darkly* concludes on a note of sham optimism, with father and son speaking of God as "love, love in all its forms", *Winter Light* tackles the loss of religious faith more directly, by unfolding in a liturgical atmosphere. Pastor Tomas Ericsson celebrates Communion in his parish church, but no longer believes in the rituals he performs. Remorse concerning his dead wife and his present mistress brings him to the verge of a breakdown. He must continue to practise his office as vicar, but comes to recognise that the fragile contact between one human being and another counts for infinitely more than the hollow litanies he indites Sunday after Sunday.

The Silence, much more adventurous in *mise en scène* than either of its predecessors, is one of Bergman's greatest works. Seamless in form, with every composition, every gesture, every word resounding to maximum effect, the film isolates its three main characters in a baroque hotel. Even they do not know where they are; the language is impenetrable, and there are intimations of war. The civilised fetters fall away; bored, each of the two sisters indulges her fancy—for the one an arid masturbation, for the other a restless coupling with an anonymous barman. Looking on is the child of one of the women, a boy who makes friends with an aged servant and with a troupe of dwarves amid the endless corridors of the hotel. Human beings are reduced to creatures of absurdity in *The Silence.* In the shadow of the Apocalypse, they can but rend one another and reach out in a desperate plea for physical contact. Bergman's editing, and the uniform milky greyness with which Sven Nykvist imbues his cinematography, give *The Silence* the texture of a dream—of a nightmare—in which God is so absent that even the sight of a tank, pausing on its painful progress through the town square, acts as a sign of some external power. If God disappears, man will seek him out in symbols.

Even more experimental and challenging was Bergman's next major film of the decade, *Persona* (1966), which the director wanted to entitle simply *Cinematography*, but needless to say the producer was aghast.

Ingrid Thulin and Gunnel Lindblom in *The Silence*.

Purity of expression achieves its absolute height in this film, in which nothing is quite as it appears. For every action there is a reaction, every question finds a question flung in answer. A nurse goes to an island with a famous actress who has suddenly become silent, just dried up in the middle of a performance on stage. Alone with each other, the young women gradually change roles. The more the nurse relates the details of her own private life, the more control the actress assumes. Like the psychologist, C.G. Jung, Bergman is probing beneath the *persona* (the Latin word for mask) into the cellar of the subconscious where resides the true *alma* (or soul-image; Alma is also the name of the nurse).

Bergman had come upon the island Fårö, to the north of Gotland in the Baltic, when scouting locations for *Through a Glass Darkly,* and fell in love with its barren shorelines, its ancient outcrops of stone, and the privacy that it could offer a celebrity like himself. Throughout the 1960's, he shot his most thoughtful pictures on Fårö, and the neutral landscape impinges on the tone and mood of each film. In *Persona,* it emphasises the deracination of the two women, the nurse from her hospital and the actress from her stage. In *Hour of the Wolf* ("Vargtimmen", 1968), it acts as a refuge of a demoniac breed of men and women, who suck into their power the hapless artist, Johan Borg, who lives in frugal solitude with his wife, Alma. Like many other Bergman figures of the period, Johan is a fugitive from his recent past, which now invades his psyche and sends him into the nether regions of insanity. *Hour of the Wolf* is an obvious tribute to the work of E.T.A. Hoffman, and to *The Magic Flute* in particular. Masonic references abound, but dominant above all is the theme of the vampire, a predator in human form who feeds on the blood of his victim by night, just as an audience feeds on the artist in the spotlight.

The primary idiom in Swedish cinema of the 1960's was political in tone, and even such a private artist as Ingmar Bergman found himself drawn to contemporary issues, dealing with them in a quasi-realistic manner, although he did not fall into the trap of producing mere tracts —of which there were several, among them *Deserter USA* (directed by Lars Lambert and Olle Sjögren in 1969), which describes the arrival and settling in Sweden of three American soldiers who have gone AWOL rather than serve in Vietnam.

Bergman aroused a hornets' nest with *Shame* ("Skammen", 1968). The conflict in southeast Asia had already "leaked" into *Persona,* where for several seconds the audience shares Liv Ullmann's shock at the TV pictures of a Buddhist monk setting light to his body in a crowded street. But *Shame* could not be interpreted in any manner other than as a private artist's expression of anguish and panic in the face of war. Not the thermo-nuclear holocaust that so alarms the fisherman in *Winter Light,* but the war that destroys the small family, that sets friend against friend, and that seems to lack all motivation.

A scene from *Persona* with Bibi Andersson and Liv Ullmann.

On an unidentified Baltic island, Jan and Eva (played by those stalwarts of Bergman's cinema in the late 1960's, Max von Sydow and Liv Ullmann) are members of a chamber orchestra who are holing up in a primitive cottage, perhaps because of the war on the mainland, or perhaps because of some nameless offence. They co-exist in a kind of armed neutrality; Eva is frustrated by her partner's petty-mindedness and lack of fibre, and Jan is slipping down a spiral of despair. His decline is accelerated by the revelation of Eva's infidelity with an old friend.

Shame uncovers the callousness of human beings in times of crisis.

Members of the small island community switch sides as the war grows more intense. The local doctor becomes a cynical bastard. Quislings are everywhere. Yet Bergman's refusal to blame one side or the other, to identify the source of the conflict, provoked the anger of Swedish intellectuals, such as Sara Lidman who condemned Bergman for granting "the contemporary Western intelligentsia total freedom from responsibility for Vietnam by turning this war into a metaphysical issue." But others admired Bergman's almost quaint belief that art could influence the world, and among these was the distinguished writer Lars Forssell, who wrote in "BLM" that *Shame* was one of "the most interesting and most significant films" Bergman had made.

As well as making a disturbing contribution to the debate about Vietnam, Bergman tried his hand at television drama, with *The Rite,* also known as *The Ritual* ("Riten", 1969), a chamber play featuring four performers—Ingrid Thulin, Gunnar Björnstrand, Anders Ek, and Erik Hell. Once again the artist is in the dock, although Bergman rarely holds his "artist" personalities in a pretentious light; they are mere entertainers, whose spectacle is composed of sleight-of-hand and jiggery-pokery, as *The Face* had demonstrated. But he still prefers them to the hated representatives of authority, like the judge in *The Rite,* who with his petty-mindedness, body-odour, and snide desires, is eventually despatched by those he seeks to harass.

Social and political films

Film-makers in Sweden have been prompted, like everyone, by impulses from either within or beyond their own country. During the 1960's, however, a conspicuous proportion of the new directors drew their inspiration from social conditions in Sweden—and from political issues prevailing outside the Nordic area. Fantasy took second place to a jarring grainy realism that sought to use film if not quite as agit-prop then certainly as an essay form, a vehicle for comment on injustice and corruption.

Few of the films in this idiom could match the ferocity of the most challenging political films of the period, by directors like Francesco

Rosi or Constantin Costa-Gavras. Some were of interest merely on account of their subject-matter. On the domestic front, the insecurity and aggressivity of the younger generation came under the microscope. Jan Halldoff, whose symbiosis with those of his own age was evident in such works as *Life's Just Great* ("Livet är stenkul", 1967) and *Ola & Julia* (released later the same year), came to maturity with two sharply-contrasted views of young people. *The Corridor* ("Korridoren, 1968) focuses on the moral difficulties of a freshly qualified doctor, who is tossed into hospital routine only to find himself sharing the social and psychological troubles of his patients. Crumbling under pressures both public and private, Per Ragnar's young M.D. retreats into the relative safety of the research unit.

Far more punishing is *A Dream of Freedom* ("En dröm om frihet", 1969), inspired by a police case of the mid-1960's. Two young criminals, from different social milieux, join together to rob a bank. During the escape, they are stopped by a police car, and one of the officers is killed. The fugitives reach Copenhagen, where they splurge part of their loot, but are then forced to hide once again in Sweden. Their capture is a grim affair in a snow-shrouded field, with a police helicopter sweeping down and giving the scene the dimensions of a hunt. Halldoff tells his story slickly, but lacks the major director's ability to examine the reasons behind the action. Yet the attraction of crime for young people in such a balanced and well-funded society as Sweden remains perplexing to artists and authorities alike.

Five years earlier, Vilgot Sjöman had adapted the sensational book, *491,* by Lars Görling, in a clear challenge to the social welfare system. Six youthful delinquents are placed together in an apartment as some kind of obscure "experiment" by an elderly welfare inspector and a young social worker. The tension among the delinquents reaches a combustible level long before some of them take up with a girl (played by Lena Nyman) and humiliate and exploit her sexual appeal—culminating in a notorious sequence involving her "rape" by an Alsatian dog. In this quasi-documentary, Sjöman passes a harsh judgement on the supervisors of the Welfare Board, who are seen to be more corrupt than the youths they control. Probation becomes a punishment, and boredom a breeding-ground for violence and perversion.

In 1969, Sjöman made a companion piece to *491*, entitled *You're Lying* ("Ni ljuger"), which exposed the soul-destroying conditions prevailing in Swedish prisons—mocked by the right-wing press both at home and abroad as being little more than holiday camps. Sjöman, again resorting to an unadorned documentary style, traces the efforts of one man to rehabilitate a chance acquaintance whose addiction to alcohol (in the face of miserable private relationships) leads him to crime and a two-year spell in Långholmen jail. Sjöman describes the prisoner's eagerness to paint and try his hand at poetry, positive features by comparison with the numbing hostility of the prison authorities.

Only ten days after the release of Sjöman's film in November 1969, an even more scathing film opened in Stockholm. Lasse Forsberg's *The Assault* ("Misshandlingen") owes as much to its leading character, played by Knut Petersen, as to its director. Crude as a slap in the face, *The Assault* makes no attempt to clothe its fury in civilised conversation. The arguments are loud and pugnacious. Knut is arrested after punching a company director on the jaw. The cause? The director's Jaguar car strikes Knut as an objectionable symbol of the upper-class stranglehold on society. At first the authorities treat Knut with patronising concern. Social researchers and psychiatrists question him about his background, but are baffled when Knut's skilful responses fail to give them the traditional explanations for violent conduct. Exasperated, they confine Knut to an institution where, in some terrifying final shots, he is thrust into a straitjacket. Society has assimilated yet another of its rebels.

The Assault forces the spectator to examine the issues rather than to side with the leading character. Knut is so abrasive a personality that he would antagonise most audiences, but that does not diminish the responsibility of society for either his behaviour or his destiny. Psychiatric care policy is demonstrated here to be too bland, too complacent, for it to be effective. The fact that Forsberg invested much of his own

Lasse Forsberg's *The Assault*, with Knut Petersen.

money into the production, combined with the raw graininess of the 16 mm images, helps to account for the impact that *The Assault* had on Swedish critics and social workers.

Although the small screen has never proved a fruitful source of art in Sweden (by comparison with Britain or the Federal Republic of Germany), it has from time to time taken risks that the film industry would decline. A social diatribe that also relied on shrewd humour to defuse its audience's built-in prejudice appeared on Swedish television in 1966. Entitled *The Grafter* ("Myglaren") it was made by Jan Myrdal—son of the famous couple, Alva and Gunnar Myrdal—and Rune Hassner. The repellent, 40-year-old man at the centre of this film is married with children. He works in a huge office block, surrounded by computers and complaisant colleagues. With a weasel's ingenuity, he sets his sights on a seat in Parliament, and Hassner and Myrdal follow his outrageous progress, as he wines and dines influential people and then casts them aside once they have outlived their usefulness. He is the perfect embodiment of a modern civil servant, living off the fat of his fellows while less astute members of society work on until the early hours of the morning. The most frightening implication of *The Grafter* is that in no other form of society would our friend have been able to rise to prominence in quite the same way. Only in modern Swedish society could he use taxpayer's money to bribe his way to power; only in the socio-political climate prevailing at the time could his very insignificance be projected to his own advantage.

The documentary factor

The *cinéma-vérité* movement in France exerted a powerful influence on Swedish documentarists during the 1960's. Both *The Grafter* and *The Assault* are charged with a spontaneity that a studio-made production could never achieve. So too is *They Call Us Misfits* ("Dom kallar oss mods", 1968), shot by two former students of the Swedish Film Institute's Film School, Stefan Jarl and Jan Lindquist. The camera follows two homeless youths, Kenta and Stoffe (actual personalities), during a few days in Stockholm. They drift from one bar to another, trying to squeeze some cheer from their daily round. Work is anathema to them. They sleep in doorways in the old part of the city (but so did Ingmar Bergman for a while in the early 1940's), until in the concluding sequence they are picked up by the police and driven away—to what? The directors declared that "Kenta and Stoffe are two unusually alive human beings in their late 'teens who, because of their indomitable need to live, are refused a place in the welfare structure, who will certainly be massacred in this society, which hasn't counted on having any marginal groups."

In a chilling sequel made almost a decade later, *A Respectable Life*

Eric M. Nilsson, one of the driving forces behind FilmCentrum.

("Ett anständigt liv", 1979), Stefan Jarl recounted the fate of Kenta and Stoffe, one of whom had died from an overdose of drugs—in real life.

The proliferation of political films in Sweden at the end of the 1960's coincided with the mood of unrest throughout Western Europe and the United States, due in part to the Vietnam war, but more profoundly to an ideological discontent shared by intellectuals and workers alike—forces that rarely unite but, when they do, threaten even the most entrenched of institutions.

In 1968, an organisation known as FilmCentrum was launched in Sweden, as a distribution point for documentaries, animated films and

From *The White Game*, filmed in Båstad in 1968.

other underprivileged productions that had been rejected by the Swedish Film Institute. Instead of sending their work to the traditional outlets of film clubs, student societies and artistic associations of various types, FilmCentrum's members—all film-makers themselves—took it to social organisations, trade unions, comprehensive schools and the like. Names that can be mentioned in connection with FilmCentrum include: Stefan Jarl, Jan Lindquist, Eric M. Nilsson, Louise O'Konor, not forgetting the most active organiser of all, Carl Henrik Svenstedt, who was anxious for FilmCentrum to stand as an alternative to the rapidly increasing power of the Film Institute and who was to develop from a critic into a competent documentalist in his own right. FilmCentrum may not have fostered any neglected masterpieces, but, like parallel bodies in the Netherlands and the United States, it attracted several of the period's most disenchanted young film-makers as well as those bent on experimentation with the media.

Folkets Bio was another alternative organisation that developed out of necessity during this period. Like FilmCentrum, it was animated by political commitment, but over the years it has championed films of many different kinds that have been neglected by the major distributors. Folkets Bio has ensured that good films reach a wider audience, in the countryside and small towns of Sweden, achieving results comparable with those of the well-known Dutch organisation, Film International. In 1983, Folkets Bio was awarded a special "Gold Bug" by the Swedish Film Institute in recognition of its pioneering efforts in the distribution field.

Such groups also compelled the Film Institute to adopt a more liberal policy, especially when prominent directors like Bo Widerberg were involved—as happened in 1968 with the documentary entitled *The White Game* ("Den vita sporten"). Sweden had long been in the forefront of world antagonism to the white settlers' regime in Rhodesia, and when a Davis Cup tennis match was scheduled between Sweden and Rhodesia in the bourgeois resort of Båstad, a pack of thirteen colleagues in the film world decided to record the demonstrations that had been forecast. They included not only Widerberg, but also the talented cinematographer Jörgen Persson, and younger figures who would make their mark as directors in the late 1970's and early 1980's, such as Ingela Romare and Lennart Malmer.

The interview material in *The White Game* pales beside the reportage of the violence at Båstad. Demonstrators blocked the gates to the courts, and the police used teargas, water cannon, and baton charges to disperse them. The match, however, was cancelled. The historian, comparing dates, finds that the Cannes Film Festival was brought to a halt a few days later by the disturbances in France. The causes were different, but the sense of spontaneous anger against blind authority was consis-

Lena Granhagen and Per Myrberg in Johan Bergenstråhle's *Made in Sweden.*

tent to all these incidents. At no other time in Swedish history has the nation's conscience collided so heavily with its avowed neutrality in world affairs.

Not all directors were willing to let the events and issues speak for themselves. In *Made in Sweden* (1969), Johan Bergenstråhle constructs a visually exotic and well-acted study of corruption. From the press conference at the start to the press conference at the end, the film is probing, questioning, pointing at its audience with an accusing finger. All Swedes, it seems to declare, are accessories to the tycoons who invest in South America, Africa, and the Far East, in order to "help" the developing countries. A young journalist is assigned to investigate a magnate named Magnus Rud (played by Max von Sydow), who is engaged in a clandestine operation to sell arms to the Vietnamese guerrillas. Nothing wrong with helping the guerillas; but that is not Rud's motive, he wants money and power.

Hideous scenes of malnutrition in the streets of India and Cambodia haunt the journalist and challenge the conventional poster picture of the East that tourist agencies so glibly display. A protracted cock fight becomes a stunning metaphor for the fight for survival—in business, in art, in Vietnam. A group of anti-war demonstrators move down a busy street shrouded in black cloaks and white masks, reminding one of medieval penitents and proving more eloquent in their comparative silence than a screaming mob. Yet *Made in Sweden* is shot through with a sense of frustration. The dishonesty can be exposed, but it thrives all the same. At least, as one old man tells the journalist's girlfriend in an interview, today's generation is more aware than any of its predecessors of what is happening in the world at large.

But then credit should be accorded to a member of the older guard, Arne Sucksdorff, for his commitment to the cause of the poor and the exploited of Rio de Janeiro. In *My Home Is Copacabana* ("Mitt hem är Copacabana", 1965) his lyrical montage dissolves the traditional barriers between fiction and documentary, painting the daily life of the slums perched high above the luxurious beaches of Rio. Most of the kids are orphans. They survive on their sense of humour and animal cunning. They sleep under newspapers in boats and along the shore. The kites they fly so often are symbols of life itself and its aspirations, just as they are in Widerberg's films. The kite becomes *part* of the child, so that he will clutch the string even in the worst fights. The natural tensions—the squabbles, the peccadilloes—are shown by Sucksdorff to be the inevitable consequence of the children's empiric existence.

"Wild children are to be found all over the world," said Sucksdorff at the time of the film's release. "But I wanted to awaken sympathy for these wonderful children, eleven years old, who know more about the seamy side of life than many of us do when we lie down and die." Buñuel, for one, would not agree with this idealistic view, and *My*

Home Is Copacabana is almost cloying by comparison with the Spanish director's *Los Olvidados*.

Widerberg's *The Ådalen Riots* (1969) invites the same ambivalent reaction. The subject – the shooting of five workers by mounted police during a strike march in the northern Swedish district of Ådalen in the depression year of 1931 – could not be worthier. But Widerberg renders it in the same gentle colours and romantic idiom as *Elvira Madigan*. He weaves a fictional pattern into the film. There is a subdued Romeo and Juliet theme running through the story, as a worker's son falls in love with his employer's daughter. When the girl becomes pregnant, her mother takes her to Stockholm for an abortion – the symbol of the void between the classes.

Widerberg knows how to exploit his summer imagery. Early scenes show children playing in the empty yards, a makeshift orchestra copying a Duke Ellington jazz fantasy ... But the tone darkens as the workers and their children try, like the Czechs in 1968, to achieve a non-violent solution by deflecting the sunlight from fragments of mirror into the soldier's eyes. The beauty of the landscape adds an undeniably obscene dimension to the violence that ensues. The soundtrack is filled with the cries of felled men, the screams of the women, and then the wail of the factory hooters announcing the tragedy to the surrounding villages. The final part of the film is a monody to the lost men, punctuated by a single damning question: "We do the shooting," says the guard to the works manager, "but who paid for the ammunition?"

Two new talents emerge

The revolution in Swedish film during this decade threw up two further talents, the one as analytical as a geophysicist, the other as fey as J.M. Barrie or W.B. Yeats.

Jonas Cornell launched his career with a comedy, *Hugs and Kisses* that tasted like a dry martini; Kjell Grede arrived with *Hugo and Josephine,* an engaging study of childhood fancies. Each man then proceeded to reveal his true personality. Cornell mapped out the contours of a contemporary marital drama in *Like Night and Day* while Grede in

Jonas Cornell's *Like Night and Day* with Claire Wikholm and Agneta Ekmanner.

the same year directed *Harry Munter,* an extraordinary quasi-fable featuring a hero who looked like Buster Keaton and behaved like a disciple of Christ.

Jonas Cornell

The white-walled interiors, and the mannequin's elegance of Agneta Ekmanner, already gave a clue in *Hugs and Kisses* ("Puss & Kram", 1967) to Jonas Cornell's cerebral attitude to aesthetics. The comedy itself, however, is delightfully astringent, setting three characters against one another in a diverting competition for love's elusive benefits. John, a bohemian writer kicked out by an irate mistress, nestles into the *ménage* of Max and Eva, whose harmonious existence is soon shown to be skin-deep. As John, like some third party in a Pinter play, disrupts the marriage, emotions are moved around like chessmen. *Hugs and Kisses* is neither farce nor melodrama, but both these elements make sporadic appearances on the horizon; and there is a wild, surrealistic party in the apartment that changes the tone disconcertingly towards the finale, featuring a quartet of children as precocious as Buñuel's beggars.

Cornell's major work, *Like Night and Day* ("Som natt och dag", 1969), also depicts life as a chic game, but the tone is more severe, in keeping with its study of a woman involved with two doctors, the one a distinguished surgeon, the other an intern in his department. Susanne (Agneta Ekmanner) is a TV announcer, and marries the surgeon with alacrity because he represents monied prestige and this gives her the chance to change her identity. But she steps into a prison: the surgeon's villa outside Stockholm resembles a mausoleum; his son by a former marriage looks on Susanne with suspicion; and she is left to cash the bonds at the bank each month while her husband travels to conferences abroad.

Cornell observes these characters in the same way as the surgeon examines his slides or X-rays, refusing to indulge their emotional implications. He is the first director in Sweden to bring home the aseptic chillness of modern banks, office blocks, and hospital labs. In the opening shots, Susanne and her young lover, Rikard, are seen strolling through a neatly tended cemetery, hinting at the couple's discontentment with their place in life. At the end, as the camera climbs above the Drottningholm Park, Susanne is a disconsolate figure among the symmetrical paths and fountains. She has tried to move into a new position within the social structure, but she has merely stepped to one side, finding solitude where she craved security and a private dream life.

Cornell, one feels, allies to his cinematic talent a flair for architecture, while most directors rely on literature as the source of their idioms. He remained as much an outsider in the Swedish New Wave as

Kjell Grede's sensitive film, *Hugo and Josephine*.

Alain Resnais did in the French cinema of the late 1950's and early 1960's, and like Resnais his career has never quite gathered momentum through the years.

Kjell Grede

Kjell Grede can claim credit for producing the first of what has proved to be a valuable and enjoyable stream of Swedish films about children. *Hugo and Josephine* ("Hugo och Josefin", 1967) is one those experiences that offers equal pleasure to youngsters and adults. Occasionally the grown-up spectator can interpret the facts that Hugo and Josephine

Harry Munter, with Jan Nielsen in the title role.

can only absorb with curiosity (such as the boy's references to his father's being in prison, probably as a conscientious objector to military service). The source of the film is the work of Maria Gripe, who with Astrid Lindgren is the best loved of Swedish children's authors. "Before it opened," says Grede, "I showed the film to two children. One said afterwards it was fun because it was like a Sunday morning when one lies in bed and experiences a lot of things and one does not know if one is awake or in a dream."

This comment casts some light on Grede's more complex, second film, *Harry Munter* (1969), which opened just eleven days before the end of the decade. Harry (Jan Nielsen) combines the gifts of engineer, dreamer, and healer. Living quietly with his parents, this young man impresses all around him with his courage (lying beneath a train as it thunders over the track), his supernatural abilities (appearing to "walk on water" as he stands on stilts in a mist-shrouded lake), and his unquenchable tenderness, which helps people like his friend Manne to combat cancer. Harry's courage also extends to other areas, such as refusing to go to the United States with his family when offered a lavish contract by a company eager to exploit his talents as an inventor. Harry floats free of everyday concerns, and thus proves a lodestone to small children, who gather round him as though fascinated to find an adult who shares their innocence. Timid and confused, Harry Munter is both delighted by the wonders of the natural world and depressed by its inherent sadness. In him co-exist the tensions and yearnings of a gener-ation wanting to care for the halt and the lame, wanting to dream of a better world, and dimly aware of the intrinsic beauty of a Sweden that with each year becomes more suffused with influences from the United States. And in his wistful gaze may be detected the dying hopes of the generation of '68.

So a decade burned out, with a return to the fantasy and bucolic vistas of the classic Swedish cinema.

The Most Recent Wave

The 1970's began auspiciously for Swedish cinema. The sleek new "Film House", conceived by Harry Schein as a power centre for everything from production (its massive basement contains two sound stages) to exhibition (two capacious theatres), cost some 4 billion kronor and became operative in 1970. Jan Troell's diptych based on the novels of Vilhelm Moberg, *The Emigrants* ("Utvandrarna", 1971) and *The New Land* ("Nybyggarna", 1972), had suffered prolonged birth pangs, but when the films eventually opened they were hailed by critics and public alike as being an admirable testament to the hardship, adventure, and challenges endured by the 19th century Swedish smallholders who had sailed across the Atlantic to find new pastures in the Mid-west of the United States. Troell's fondness for the characters and his eye for landscape and the poetic image, were enhanced by the 70 mm spaciousness of the work. No surprise, therefore, that *The Emigrants* was nominated for numerous Academy Awards in Hollywood, including Best Picture.

Since 1970 the way has been open to an inordinate number of new and neophyte directors in Sweden. Failure at the box-office has by no means ensured extinction for all too many of these film-makers, many of whom do not have the visual or dramatic talent required to create intriguing screen art. An irony of the 1970's was that one of its best achievements, *Sven Klang's Combo*, was made by a group rather than by an individual *auteur*.

Modern Swedish society in film

Swedish cinema has become increasingly political in tone over the past fifteen years. Artists have fought against the encroaching power of the State, which had become a kind of mega-authority established by the collective energy of individuals over several decades, and yet which

Leaving home for a new continent, a scene from *The Emigrants*.

now seems to ride roughshod over liberties that those individuals have long cherished. The hairline cracks in the Swedish economy have widened into fissures during the 1970's and 1980's. Living standards have remained stable at best; the value of the Swedish krona has sunk against other currencies. The Swedish State's worst sin, however, has been its indifference towards its citizens' real personal needs and the ever tightening net of regulations.

Few Swedish film-makers of the past fifteen years have been able, however, to chart this malaise in ways that are both entertaining and barbed. Political cinema has either remained in the wings (the work of

Stefan Jarl.

Stefan Jarl's topical documentary on the pollution of the environment, *Nature's Revenge*.

FilmCentrum, for instance), or has been restricted to documentaries (of which Stefan Jarl's *Nature's Revenge* is one of the finest examples). Widerberg and Sjöman flourished in the 1960's, but the new generation seems more interested in pursuing private obsessions than in reforming society. Carl Johan Seth and Hans Dahlberg, though, did make a creditable foray into this genre with *Seven Girls* ("Om sju flickor", 1974). In an idyllic rural setting, girls who have sidestepped the regulations of society are brought into line. A new assistant becomes on his arrival the transformer for the private fears and complexes of all the girls; and, learning from Kenneth Loach's quiet, observant style, the directors eschew melodrama, sex, and calculated violence. Each of these young women is a distinct personality. Frustration—perhaps a lack of faith— binds their seven souls together, and the film's indecisive ending bequeaths the problem to the audience, to the materialist society.

Certain gifted figures in the Swedish cinema have opted for indirect criticism of modern systems, housing their anger within a more traditional narrative structure. Gunnel Lindblom, for long and unjustly saddled with the reputation of a sex symbol after playing the sensual sister in Bergman's *The Silence,* has brought forth two interesting works. *Paradise Place* ("Paradistorg", 1976) uses the family gathering at a summer-house as the catalyst for an exposé of the emotional insecurity lurking beneath bourgeois gloss. Birgitta Valberg and Sif Ruud are among the predominantly female cast, and work hard to create persuasive, sympathetic characters. The schematism of this film, however, handicaps it by comparison with Gunnel Lindblom's second work for the screen, *Sally and Freedom* ("Sally och friheten", 1981), in which the infrastructure of Swedish society is flayed with quite startling verisimilitude. Here abortions may be obtained as easily as teeth removed. Sally (Ewa Fröling) breaks up with her husband in a vague quest for freedom, but finds that she leaps almost immediately into an identical prison. Sally is too weak and immature to achieve her goal and at the end she starts with yet another clean slate, as she aborts for the second time, just one in a line of beds being trundled down to the operating theatre. In Sweden, the film seems to be whispering, science and tech-

Ewa Fröling as Sally in *Sally and Freedom*.

Gunnel Lindblom.

nology have taken care of everything; but nobody quite comprehends that little thing called love.

Although he has not developed into a major film director, Bergenstråhle has continued to provoke the Establishment with each new film. *For Your Pleasure* ("Slumrande toner", 1977) consists of a series of impressions and tableaux, as a small group of actors travels through Finland under the command of an irascible and lecherous boss. There are echoes here of the early Bergman, with the theme of the performers as objects of abuse in the eyes of a philistine public (although the irony is that the audiences are composed of underprivileged and handicapped members of society, even lunatics).

Stig Björkman, an architect turned film critic and then director, has also embedded in his work a vein of social criticism. The most impressive of Björkman's films to date has been *The White Wall* ("Den vita väggen", 1975), which describes a typical day in the life of an "emancipated" Scandinavian woman. Waking beside a strange man, applying fruitlessly for a job, trying to contact her vagrant husband, going to a gloomy dance-hall with a friend. It is a plaintive movie, almost a documentary on the individual at odds with the smooth, gleaming contours of modern Swedish society. Even if Björkman's visuals are cool and uninviting, like an abandoned dinner, his film contains a masterly performance by Harriet Andersson as the central victim of that Nordic complaint, loneliness.

One of the most acute problems of recent years in Sweden has been the situation facing immigrants. By far the largest foreign minority are the Finns, and in Jon Lindström's *Homeward in the Night* ("Hemåt i natten", 1977) the perennial nightmare of the migrant worker is encapsulated. Harri, the Finnish welder who seeks sex and fortune in Sweden, might as well be a Turk in the Federal Republic of Germany or an Italian in Switzerland. The pressures of a foreign language and native hostility have brought better men than Harri to their knees. When Harri returns to Finland, he finds himself a spiritual alien there, too.

The prejudice towards foreign workers has emerged in other Swedish films, the best of which is probably Johan Bergenstråhle's *Foreigners*

("Jag heter Stelios", 1972), which portrays the strengths and weaknesses of a Greek community in Stockholm. By retaining their ethnic traditions, these immigrants can shield themselves from the contempt and superciliousness displayed towards them at every turn, in streets, offices, and factories alike. Bergenstråhle's earlier *A Baltic Tragedy* ("Baltutlämningen", 1970) had touched a similar nerve with its resurrection of an unforgivable miscarriage of justice after the Second World War, when Baltic refugees were extradited from Sweden to face retribution from the hand of the Soviet authorities.

Glancing back

Nostalgia for the past has coloured much Swedish cinema of recent years. Apart from *The Emigrants,* the late 19th and early 20th centuries have featured in Ingvar Skogsberg's *City of My Dreams* ("Mina drömmars stad", 1977), based on Fogelström's series about Stockholm, with its Dickensian detail of poverty, and a splendid portrait by Peter Lindgren of the boorish father; and Anja Breien's *Games of Love and Loneliness* ("Den allvarsamma leken", 1977), a remake of the 1945 screen version of Hjalmar Söderberg's novel. Brought into the project at the last moment, Ms. Breien, from neighbouring Norway, treats the turn of the century tale with marked respect, but beneath the grave progression of the narrative ("And the years passed ...") there is a dark, surging current of feeling that does justice to Söderberg's recognition of that eternal clash between security and contingency in the realms of love.

The 1930's has also attracted the affections of younger directors, perhaps in an attempt to peer beneath the frivolous image of the Depression era given by the comedies that were produced at the time. Per Berglund, destined to become an inspiring producer, made his early mark with *Beyond the Line of Duty* ("Den magiska cirkeln", 1970), a film reminiscent of *Bonnie and Clyde* in its nostalgic vision of gangsterism. Swedish youths, bored to distraction in the unemployment decade, were easily tempted by the grandeur attached to criminal escapades. Ingvar, the son of a small-town outfitter—and a real-life character, only released from jail during the 1960's—uses his bizarre intelligence to bamboozle his friends into joining his "Magic Circle" until they perform one reckless outrage and murder at his bidding. The film's appeal lies in its tone of sadness predominating over anger, in its discreet reminder that society poor or (as now) rich, often presses its most gifted members into warped patterns of behaviour.

A more gentle homage to the 1930's is paid by Ingrid Thulin in her *Broken Sky* ("Brusten himmel", 1982). Seldom has a film communicated so acutely the feelings of an only child (Ms. Thulin herself, played by Susanna Käll) growing up in a pastoral environment—the walks beside the lake, the skiing across the fields to see the old grannie, with whom the girl has more rapport than with her parents. Ingrid Thulin's memories come from the far north of Sweden; those of Vilgot Sjöman are city-based, and in his own *Linus* (1979) he filters the impressions of his youth through a highly-coloured melodrama about a teenage boy's being sucked into a web of eroticism and intrigue, after witnessing a murder outside a huge, baleful building in the Stockholm of the late 1920's. Sjöman delineates this claustrophobic situation with mordant wit. The very structure of the house becomes a microcosm of the adult world, where ambition is defined by the number of steps one can climb towards wealth and an indulgence of the senses.

Although some would point to *Blushing Charlie* ("Lyckliga skitar", 1970) as the quintessential Sjöman film of the 1970's, with its cosy, smirking picture of a truck-driver's life in and around his house-boat, there is no doubt that *A Handful of Love* ("En handfull kärlek", 1974), set at the time of the General Strike in Sweden (1909), represents this maverick director's most ambitious work of the past fifteen years. The social confrontation in the film recalls Widerberg's *The Ådalen Riots.* Sjöman, however, is a rationalist where Widerberg is a romantic, and the tangled relationships in *A Handful of Love* are analysed with surgical precision. Hjördis, the working girl, is exploited by her employers, and ends by scrubbing the floors of the Communist Party HQ in Stockholm after her activist lover, Daniel, and his friends have been humbled by the failure of the strike. As always, one of the strengths of Swedish

Malin Ek and Moa Stridbeck in a tender moment from *Our Life is Now*.

cinema is its ability to produce historical films of evocative power and accuracy. The veteran art director, P.A. Lundgren, evokes the early years of the century with an innate flair for domestic detail, and the cinematography of Jörgen Persson, already celebrated for *Elvira Madigan*, endows *A Handful of Love* with a glittering surface texture.

The angst-ridden 1940's has not been a decade to attract the backward glance. Suzanne Osten's *Our Life Is Now* ("Mamma", 1983), however, is a nostalgic paean to the persistence of the director's mother, a film critic much influenced by her early experiences in Paris, who strives to reconcile the demands of being a single parent and a fledgling film-maker. *Our Life Is Now* wallows in self-gratification and a naive acceptance of French culture, but amid the banality there is a central performance by Malin Ek that flares with feminist conviction.

A decade less deserving of art, the 1950's, fared considerably better, though, in *Sven Klang's Combo* ("Sven Klangs kvintett", 1977). The music and theatre group, "October", collaborated on this remarkable film, written by Henric Holmberg, Ninne Olsson, and Stellan Olsson, who also directed. Like *American Graffiti* and *Next Stop Greenwich Village,* this unpretentious little masterpiece recognises that big emotions stem from small incidents, and that one is forever a prisoner of one's generation. In a town in southern Sweden, Sven Klang decides to enliven his dance combo with a new sax player, Lasse from Stockholm. At first all goes well, but by degrees Lasse brings into question all the rigid values—musical and social—by which the faintly supercilious Sven has set his life's course.

The appeal of the film lies in its small-town atmosphere and its vivid characterisation. One imagines that the actors were able to improvise their lines and contribute personal touches that fleshed out their roles. Their autobiographies become fiction; but fiction, as so often, also becomes fact. *Sven Klang's Combo* has unjustly been dismissed as a jazz-buff's movie. The music is excellent, but so too is the black-and-white photography of Kent Persson, and the ensemble acting of the "October" group.

Finnish-born Lars Thelestam's film *Triumph Tiger '57* ("Hempas Bar", 1976) describes the same period as *Sven Klang's Combo*—Bosse Andersson's screenplay conjures up the dour aspirations of provincial Sweden during the 1950's. Kille's big brother, Helge, returns bleak-eyed and cynical from a trip to the States. He is high on Presley and the get-rich-quick ethic. "Those who abide by the rules are the losers," he warns Kille, who is still under the avuncular influence of the Boy Scouts. While Helge bikes noisily around the ill-lit streets and seduces the local café-owner's mistress (Harriet Andersson), Kille endures a fractious relationship with his parents. Some innate goodness prevents Kille from adopting his brother's recipe for life; and in the wake of

Helge's final savage, selfish outrage, he runs out along a pier, surrounded on all sides by water, like Truffaut's Antoine Doinel at the end of *The 400 Blows,* as though the act of running itself implied the getting of wisdom.

Comedy

"Hell," quoth David Frost, "is a place where the Swedes are the comedians." Swedes do laugh as much as other nations at themselves, however; one has only to sit in a Stockholm cinema and watch the latest Gösta Ekman vehicle to realise that. But sophisticated comedy is beyond their film-makers on all but the rarest of occasions. Even Bergman, while achieving perfection with *Smiles of a Summer Night,* stumbled into embarrassing witlessness with *The Devil's Eye* and *Now About These Women/All these Women.*

Recent Swedish comedies tend to fall—sometimes collapse—into one or two categories. Firstly the more fashionable formula of the past few years involves a trio of men unnerved by their own complexes and insecurity. The women are sex objects, to be ogled and talked of in leering whispers. In this chauvinist genre, the films of Jan Halldoff, Lasse Hallström, Lasse Åberg, and Hans Iveberg are prominent. Few of them would amuse audiences outside their native shores; Åberg's work, including the enormously popular satires, *The Call-Up* ("Repmånad") and *The Charter Trip* ("Sällskapsresan") made in 1978 and 1980 respectively, rises above the norm thanks to the director's own Tati-like personality, a well-meaning klutz who stumbles through two of Sweden's hallowed rituals—military service in the reserve, and the package holiday. Hallström's *Father To Be* ("Jag är med barn", 1979) is a pleasing confection about a young man who becomes almost more expectant than his wife when it comes to a baby, and whose hilarious antics poke sly fun at the Swedish urge for equality in domestic matters. The same director's rites of passage movies, *Boy Meets Girl* ("En kille och en tjej", 1975) and *Happy We* ("Två killar och en tjej", 1983) are autobiographical in tone but lacking in bite. The insecure male threesome essential to this genre may have led to the "remaking" of the

Danish *Olsen Gang* series, by the enterprising producer, Ingemar Ejve, with Gösta Ekman and his colleagues in crime forming the notorious Jonsson Gang, congenitally incapable of bringing off a heist, in (to date) three fast-moving comedies of errors: *Beware of the Jonsson Gang* ("Varning för Jönssonligan!", 1981), directed by Jonas Cornell, *The Jonsson Gang Meets Dynamite-Harry* ("Jönssonligan och Dynamit-Harry", 1982), directed by Mikael Ekman and *The Jonsson Gang Catches Gold-fever* ("Jönssonligan får guldfeber", 1984).

The second kind of contemporary Swedish farce almost invariably involves the ubiquitous Gösta Ekman. Son of Hasse Ekman, grandson of the legendary Gösta Ekman (Ingrid Bergman's lover in *Intermezzo*), this actor goes from strength to strength. Like many comedians, he is a more intelligent player than his material might suggest—and indeed his performance in Mats Arehn's sombre tale of emotional bondage, *A Summer's Love* ("En kärlekssommar", 1979) demonstrates just that. Ekman brings the right blend of romanticism and non-conformity to the central role in Hans Dahlberg's *Walking in the Sun* ("En vandring i solen", 1979), about a debilitated journalist who travels to Cyprus with a charter group, flounders about unhappily in the sun, and is just starting to revive under the influence of a Norwegian girl courier, when an accident plunges him back into the depths of Swedish *angst*. The small miracle of *Walking in the Sun* is that it never sinks into that quagmire of self-pity that engulfs so many Swedish films. The screenplay (by Bibi Edlund, from a novel by Stig Claesson) bristles with waggish asides on the tourist habit, and Sif Ruud and Irma Christenson are delightful as two matrons who fuss over the cuckoo in their nest.

Ekman's presence invariably assures a box-office bonanza. One of his most deserved hits was *To Be a Millionaire* ("Mannen som blev miljonär", 1980), Mats Arehn's first attempt at lightweight material and a satire on the Western world's terror of terrorism, with Ekman and Björn Gustafsson as discombobulated criminals who kidnap the Prime Minister's daughter and her nanny.

The most rewarding symbiosis between comedian and director, however, has been the work involving Ekman and Hans Alfredson. For

Prospects look grim for Gösta Ekman in a scene from *Beware of the Jonsson Gang*.

much of his career Alfredson has teamed with his friend Tage Danielsson to create some of the finest cabaret entertainment in Scandinavia. "Hasse & Tage" has become a byword for wit that is both warm and spicy for the Swedes, and the partners' films have enjoyed almost as much popularity. *The Apple War* ("Äppelkriget", 1971) whipped up the most stir, although during the 1960's they produced concoctions as varied as *Swedish Pictures* ("Svenska bilder", 1964), *Go Ashore* ("Att angöra en brygga", 1965), both of which featured a young Ekman in minor roles, as did *The Apple War,* where he played a PR man. When Alfredson and Danielsson gave him the lead in *The Man Who Gave Up Smoking* ("Mannen som slutade röka", 1972), however, Gösta Ekman revealed a sense of timing and a range of comic talent to enthrall the Swedish audience. In this and in his subsequent triumphs for the team, *Egg, Egg, A Hardboiled Story* ("Ägget är löst!", 1974), *Let the Prisoners Go, for It's Spring* ("Släpp fångarne loss−det är vår!", 1976), *The Adventures of Picasso* ("Picassos äventyr", 1978), and *Refuse* ("Sopor", 1981), Ekman compensated for his lack of facial or bodily idiosyncrasies with a frenetic energy and a capacity for adopting chameleon-like disguises. As satire, the work of Alfredson and Danielsson is delivered more often with the axe than the rapier, and it was perhaps inevitable that Alfredson should peel off on his own and embark on more ambitious schemes.

Experimental cinema has never flourished in the orthodox soil of the Swedish film industry, and so it was only from his position of box-office strength that Alfredson could tackle such a bold and pessimistic project as *The Simple-Minded Murderer* ("Den enfaldige mördaren", 1982), which nevertheless drew more than 400,000 spectators. Made with palpable conviction and a magisterial control both of pace and players, *The Simple-Minded Murderer* revives the morality play tradition of *The Road to Heaven* and *The Seventh Seal*. Stellan Skarsgård won the Silver Bear for Best Actor at the Berlin Festival for his role as the simpleton with the harelip who is exploited by an evil magnate (played by Alfredson himself) and who eventually slaughters him at the bidding of three "Angels". Swedes swear by the film, but unless one accepts the Nordic obsession with humiliation, it may be difficult not to mock the comicbook infamy of the factory-owner, the condescending view of the "Idiot", and the apparition of the Angels striding with wings rampant through the streets of a sleepy Swedish town. Two years later, Alfredson returned to comedy with *P & B,* again set in the 1930's and again featuring Stellan Skarsgård. These two films have proved Hans Alfredson to be among the most assured and imaginative film-makers of his generation, even if his work seems to have difficulty in crossing the seas.

Another Swedish comedian who has clearly aimed at more than mere farce is Allan Edwall. Without doubt a gifted dramatic actor (viz. *Win-*

Stellan Skarsgård in *The Simple-Minded Murderer*.

ter Light, Here Is Your Life, and *The Emigrants*), Edwall also projects immense appeal as a comic figure, sometimes in the screen versions of children's stories by Astrid Lindgren, and sometimes, as in *Loafie* ("Limpan", 1983), which he wrote, by representing the outsider, the unfortunate Swede who falls foul of the system. Edwall is one of a number of actors and actresses in Sweden who have turned their hand to directing. Over the last few years he has brought a thoughtful eye to bear on films such as *Loafie* and more recently in *Åke and His World* ("Åke och hans värld", 1984) about a six-year-old boy whose charmed existence at home is contrasted with the dangers and designs of the outside world.

Offbeat approaches

What, then, of experiments unprotected by popular stars? It is a story of protracted production schedules, budgets exceeded, and box-office ignominy. Even on the export market, the would-be visionaries of the Swedish cinema have been damned with faint praise. Some directors have never deserted their high ideals and refusal to compromise—Marianne Ahrne, for example, Kay Pollak, Stefan Jarl, Marie-Louise De Geer Bergenstråhle, Christina Olofson and Göran du Rées. Others have been unable to work further in the commercial cinema: Jösta Hagelbäck, for instance, or Roy Andersson. Others still, like Erland Josephson and Lárus Óskarsson, find their work greeted with enthusiastic reviews and few paying customers.

Roy Andersson, whose *A Swedish Love Story* ("En kärlekshistoria", 1970) had won the hearts of young audiences throughout Sweden, with its unaffected, innocuous image of the teenage generation, spent several years of the 1970's striving to complete *Giliap*, which eventually appeared in 1976. Thommy Berggren arrives as a waiter at a saturnine hotel on the Swedish coast. "Passing through?" asks another member of the staff. "Yes, you could say that," responds Berggren in one of the film's resonant exchanges. Hotel and restaurant are bathed in a sepulchral hush, even at the height of the lunch hour. The manager is confined to a wheelchair and complains interminably about the staff and the world in general. Real time elapses with painful inertia. For over an hour there is no scene in daylight; *Giliap* unfolds in a twilight zone of cavernous rooms and maudlin bars. When occasionally his characters threaten to escape the prevailing lethargy, Andersson fades

Roy Andersson's
A Swedish Love Story.

out, or cuts to an image of stillness. The style is not sufficiently rich to sustain an audience's interest to the end. Rarely, however, have the flotsam and jetsam of the Swedish welfare state been so honestly and intriguingly described.

More kinetic (thanks largely to the photography by Sten Holmberg), Jösta Hagelbäck's *The Emperor* ("Kejsaren", 1979) constitutes a spare, unrelenting vision of the handicapped, and the prejudice they excite, although as with *The Simple-Minded Murderer* there is a whiff of condescension about the film's attitude to human suffering. This criticism could not be levelled at *Near and Far Away* ("Långt borta och nära"

1977), which deals with the affliction known as mutism. Mania is a social worker who joins the staff of a mental hospital and becomes fascinated by a patient there, a mutist whose blank gaze and gentle features respond to the girl's kindliness. But the stiff, joyless conduct of the hospital staff blights this natural, tender shoot of hope. Marianne Ahrne's warm and generous direction comprehends unerringly that feelings must always outweigh scientific achievement, and in her second film, *Roots of Grief* ("Frihetens murar", 1979) she again focuses on an outsider befriended by an affectionate woman. Ms. Ahrne's "experiment" is not registered in technical terms—the *mise en scène* of both films is pedestrian—so much as in emotional tension. Her study of an Argentinian immigrant blundering into the crass, narrow-minded midst of Swedish petty bourgeois society, radiates a glow of feeling, a commitment to the relief of human agony that is quite without parallel in Scandinavian cinema.

Lasse Forsberg, whose *The Assault* remains one of the bravest films of the 1960's, has continued to struggle along a difficult path. *Robert and Fanny* ("Måndagarna med Fanny", 1977) X-rays a misanthropic, middle-aged individual, easily provoked, seething with inchoate resentment against the shabby genteelism of married life and routine work. Crushed by a domineering father in youth, awkward with women, Robert has neither inherited nor acquired the gift of compassion. *Robert and Fanny* lacks sympathetic characters, yet still emerges from its bleakness as a tender film. The locations (a ravaged strip of coast, a clinic enveloped by woods) ally with the powerful music to suggest the desolation of Robert's soul.

Christopher's House ("Kristoffers hus", 1980), although more complex in structure than Forsberg's earlier features, fared better in public esteem, principally on account of the alluring role it afforded Thommy Berggren. Akin to *Blow Up* in its mood of mystery and its use of a professional photographer's innate curiosity, the film gives off an ambivalent atmosphere that is just marred by a somewhat dollar-book ending.

Experiment for experiment's sake is the besetting sin of Marie-

Louise De Geer Bergenstråhle, who contributed to the screenplay and cast of her former husband Johan Bergenstråhle's *Hallo Baby* (1976), an autobiographical story of a young girl's coming to terms with her own naiveté in Stockholm's artistic circles. Never boring, *Hallo Baby* discourages interpretation; a *film à clef*, it demonstrates that pretentiousness is the Achilles heel of experiment. Marie-Louise De Geer's solo effort, *Elephant Walk* ("Barnförbjudet", 1980) presents the world as glimpsed through the eyes of a six-year-old child. The fantasy yields some arresting images, but once again the film remains too private and too self-indulgent to reach a significant audience.

The child's imagination also colours Kay Pollak's very impressive *Children's Island* ("Barnens ö", 1980). His visuals, his control of sound, his direction of players—all have a supple, visceral quality that involves the audience. *Elvis! Elvis!* (1976) was inspired by the story by Maria Gripe, but *Children's Island* becomes Pollak's exclusive property, even if P.C. Jersild's novel about an eleven-year-old boy who takes off on his own to Stockholm during the summer vacation, is a marvellous springboard for the film. Like Jersild, Pollak externalises the desires and fantasies, the fears and aspirations, of pubescent boyhood, but he endows these feelings with a mysterious glow and poetry. When Reine tries to stay underwater for as long as possible, one suffers with him, feels the thumping of the blood in one's veins and the chillness of the surrounding water. Reine's discovery of profanation, sex, jealousy, and all those other illusions and disillusions that form the process of growing up, are beautifully marshalled by Kay Pollak.

Christina Olofson and Göran du Rées, working in Gothenburg, established an early bridgehead on the western front of Swedish cinema with *The Painter* ("Målaren", 1982). Its use of music and long-shots in the telling of a melancholy tale about an industrial worker who wants to expand his artistic activity helped *The Painter* win selection for the Critic's Week at the Cannes Film Festival, no mean achievement for a Swedish production. *Where Were You Jacob?* ("Jacob—smitaren", 1983) was a catastrophe from which one hopes the Olofson-du Rées partnership can recover.

Children's Island, Kay Pollack's powerful film based on P.C. Jersild's novel.

The most compelling debut of recent years in Swedish cinema has also been the most audacious in form and content. Lárus Óskarsson, an Icelander who had graduated from the Institute of the Dramatic Arts in Stockholm, may be the finest talent born of the North this decade. Shallow critics have tarred Óskarsson's effort with the brush of Wenders, Polanski, and Antonioni, but throughout this road movie for women there are constant flashes of inspiration so enigmatic, so magical, and so impish that they evoke nothing so much as that key Swedish word for imagination that translates literally as "fantasy full". In *The Second Dance* ("Andra dansen", 1983), two women meet outside Stockholm. Jo, the younger one, gives Anna a lift in her battered Citroën. While Anna is bold and assertive, quick-thinking and shrewd, Jo lingers in the background, recording incidents with her camera. Anna dreams of a father and a legacy that might be hers; but, as in all classic road movies, the journey, not the arrival matters. In a hotel worthy of Hitchcock, an impromptu drinks party goes sour; an ugly black bird watches malevolently in a nearby room. In a bizarre, floodlit mansion, both girls dress up in ball gowns and then flee from the distraught houseowner. When the car breaks down, they take refuge in a forest cabin, only to be menaced by two horny layabouts. Finally, much shaken, they reach Anna's native smallholding in Norrland. News of death and decay is the sole reward.

Göran Nilsson and Jan Pehrsson contribute monochrome photography of the highest calibre, transmuting the virgin landscape of northern Sweden into a dream zone, in which people become dark shadows, of themselves and of their past and future. Behind the magic of *The Second Dance* lurks the eye of Lárus Óskarsson, spying on the characters, sharing their dreams, fastening on the unguarded moment, just like Jo with her Polaroid.

Among other new names to conjure with is the Finnish-born Tuija-Maija Niskanen, whose *The Farewell* ("Avskedet", 1983) was financed by Bergman's own company, Cinematograph, and strikes a remarkably mature note in its description of upper-class life in Finland before the war, with the main character, a middle-aged woman, recalling the ruthless, domineering presence of her father. Based on the life and writings of the stage producer, Viveca Bandler, *The Farewell* was also the swansong of an underrated Swedish actor, Carl-Axel Heiknert, who endowed the paterfamilias in this film with awesome authority.

Modern literature on screen

Novels have sustained much modern Swedish cinema, as in all other countries. From time to time a fine literary base can elevate the work of a journeyman director, as happened in 1974, when Jan Halldoff adapted a novel by Per Gunnar Evander, *The Last Adventure* ("Det sista äventyret"), for the screen. A young man, Jimmy (played with intelligent awareness by Göran Stangertz) is all at once appalled by the life that has been so carefully – and insensitively – mapped out for him by his parents. To his horror he finds that the outside world is just as inhibiting and exasperating as the army camp where he has been completing his national service. So he turns tail and becomes a teacher, promptly falling in love with one of his pupils. The chilling lesson of the film, however, confirms that Jimmy is as bourgeois and blinkered as his parents' generation, ready to adopt the tactics of either defence or attack. As a study of someone caught in the limbo dividing two codes of morality, *The Last Adventure* is refreshingly accurate of gaze.

Bengt Forslund, a portal figure in Swedish cinema of the last twenty years, has developed his skills as a producer, opting just once for the director's chair. His film version of Per Wästberg's superb Eternal Triangle novel, *The Air Cage* ("Luftburen", 1972), often makes the mistake of letting characters pronounce lines of dialogue directly from the literary original. Its mood, though, is beguiling, describing the three main personalities in terms cerebral yet tender, emphasising the unpalatable truth that each man, *pace* John Donne, *is* an island, despatching a stream of anguished signals in the hope of communicating with others. The film points to the ecological errors of the age – the gutting and reconstruction of central Stockholm, for example, or the pollution of the big jets descending into Arlanda.

Two other productions of the mid-1970's bore the unmistakable – and debilitating – marks of literary adaptations. Michael Meschke, better known for his work as a puppeteer, made a brave attempt to seize on film the essence of Dante's *Divine Comedy*. Entitled *Purgatorio* ("Skärseld", 1974), it manoeuvred its poetic imagery with reasonable skill, but could not evade the charge of banality. The crucial decision by Meschke and his colleague, Silvano Agosto, to set the film in a contemporary world, however hallucinatory, did not work to its advantage. Ivo Dvořák, one of the Czech émigrés who settled in Sweden after the invasion of Prague in 1968, made a worthy stab at transporting Kafka's *Metamorphosis* to the screen a year or so later, and captured the sinister mood of Prague in some grisly, grainy visuals (with agile photography by Jiří Tirl), but the most terrifying aspect of the story—the actual transmogrification of Gregor into a monstrous beetle—is missing. *Metamorphosis* ("Förvandlingen", 1976), is thus a film to admire but not to fear.

Tirl himself created a miniature jewel among Swedish films with *The Pistol* ("Pistolen", 1973). Smacking of some romantic, Chekhovian short story, this 80 minute production catches the bewitching allure of a quainter Stockholm ignored by orthodox directors. This is the quiet city one sees on Sunday morning in autumn, with the green-domed churches lined against the blue sky. There is a feeling of time lying dormant, an air of courtly elegance, a notion of loss. The Countess Alisia lives alone in a huge castle outside the city. The last of her aristocratic line, she yearns to die in a way that matches the beauty of her surroundings and her heritage. Tirl sympathises with her fate, coaxing a memorable performance from the great stage actress, Inga Tidblad, and casting an elegiac glance back at the Czechoslovakia he was compelled to leave.

Thrillers

Crime thrillers have appealed to several Swedish film-makers, although few directors have been content to dwell merely on the mechanics of the plot.

For Christer Dahl, *The Score* ("Lyftet", 1978) was a means of expressing more about the boredom of existence in Swedish society today. Its shape conforms to that of the traditional gangster movie (the source was a novel by Dahl and Lasse Strömsteudt): Kennet is an amateurish hoodlum, as the hilarious hold-up before the credits neatly shows. He views life as a raw battle between himself and the community. Choleric and inconsiderate, he exasperates every right-minded person with whom he comes in contact, including his girlfriend's parents. He's in and out of jail like a yo-yo, but the force and cogency of the film are such that one sides with this anti-hero even though Kennet flouts the ground rules of society at every turn. Kennet, the perennial misfit (based partly on Strömstedt's experiences as a convict) is the only screen Swede of recent years imbued with a real zest for life. For him "the score" remains a dream beyond his reach; there are no short cuts to the big time. Even Dustin Hoffman, an actor of similar size and style, would have been hard pressed to match the shade and texture of Anders Lönnbro's acting as Kennet.

The thriller format enabled Mats Arehn to make a trenchant comment on the Swedish attitude to the developing countries. Adapting a political suspense novel by Per Wahlöö, *The Assignment* ("Uppdraget", 1977), Arehn proceeds to show how the Swedish brand of benevolent neutrality is dismissed with scorn at the battlefronts of the contemporary world. Dalgren, a trim young diplomat, flies from Stockholm to an unnamed Latin American country in an effort to mediate between right and left in the wake of a General's assassination. Appalled by what he sees, he realises that his ethical code is completely inadequate in the face of a voracious and endemic violence. He is transfixed, like a rabbit in the gaze of a snake, by the chief of police, Behounek (Christopher Plummer), only to become aware that this man too is a born loser. Behounek has grown numb from killing, just as Dalgren has grown ineffectual from years of welfare cossetting. Arehn's film suffers from a slim budget and the hazards of recording an original soundtrack in English, but the strength of its impact is only slightly reduced.

Crime also formed the backdrop to Arehn's promising debut, *Maria* (1975), which contained ample reserves of warmth and commitment in its mundane story of an inveterate robber's relationship with an unmarried mother, trying to survive against the odds in modern Sweden.

The most satisfying thriller of the past fifteen years, however, is Bo Widerberg's *The Man on the Roof* ("Mannen på taket", 1976), by virtue of its professional panache and lack of pretension. Infinitely more authentic than Hollywood's efforts at filming the Inspector Martin Beck novels of Maj Sjöwall and Per Wahlöö, *The Man on the Roof* races past with such speed that only afterwards can one discern its attempt to analyse the symbiosis between police and public in a liberal

The Man from Mallorca (1984), Sven Wollter and Tomas von Brömssen.

and rather disillusioned democracy. In 1984, Widerberg returned, with considerable success, to the same genre, with *The Man from Mallorca* ("Mannen från Mallorca", 1984).

The return of Jan Troell

Jan Troell has endured a difficult patch since the high noon of *The Emigrants* and *The New Land*. Frustration in Hollywood *(Zandy's Bride, Hurricane)*, a private exorcism on screen *(Bang!)*, and the

129

chance to direct his dream project, *The Flight of the Eagle,* only to find himself embroiled in budgetary hassles and then damned with faint praise by the critics when his magnum opus did emerge. There is no doubt Troell is without peer in Nordic film where men in defiance of nature are concerned. *Bang!* was an honourable failure, a means of Troell's dealing with his mid-life crisis, and doing so in a film that contained surges of fantasy all the more tantalising for being so private. *The Flight of the Eagle* ("Ingenjör Andrées luftfärd", 1982), however, inspired by Per Olof Sundman's "docudrama" about the doomed journey of S.A. Andrée and two companions in search of the North Pole—in a balloon—in 1897, is much less deserving of scorn. There is more throbbing emotion in ten minutes of *The Flight of the Eagle* than in a hundred of the much-vaunted *Gandhi.* To be fair, some vital substance is lacking. It is not the length of the film, but rather the screenplay, which fails to give a crucial third dimension to any character save Andrée himself (and how Max von Sydow rises to the challenge of playing this Kiplingesque, benighted dreamer!). Out in the icy wastes, with Andrée's balloon lurching perilously on course for the North Pole, Troell revels in his element. As an anthology piece, this central segment of the film is a superb blend of crystalline photography (by Troell himself) and physical attrition. Like Scott of the Antarctic, Andrée brought a kind of noble futility to his mission. Stubborn and wilful he may be but when, companions dead, he looks about him in despair, his is the romantic gesture one secretly applauds.

Films for children

Animation and the crafting of films for children occupy a cherished place in the modern Swedish cinema. Most animators have aimed their work at a youthful audience, and Sweden has produced at least two first-class feature films in this mode during the past decade. *Dunderklumpen* from 1974, by Per Åhlin, blends live-action scenes—shot in the delightful expanses of Jämtland in the North of Sweden—with animated characters. A small boy is lured out of his home on Midsummer's Night, and his father goes in search of him. Their adventures are rather non-

Troell's most recent film, *The Flight of the Eagle*.

Three examples of successful films for children: *The Brothers Lionheart*,

descript, but the cartoon figures are enchanting, among them the gigantic "John", composed—literally—of a mountain, whose favourite pastime is plunging his slopes into the lake, and a raddled hag known for obvious reasons as Elvira Fattigan. Dunderklumpen himself is a potato-faced creature who can breathe life into toys and leads his camp-followers in a genial procession.

Peter No-Tail ("Pelle Svanslös", 1981) confirmed Stig Lasseby as a genuine talent in the animation field. The novels of Gösta Knutsson have captivated Swedish youngsters for many years, with their treatment of cats as human beings. Peter No-Tail competes with the less

Peter-No-Tail and...

...the ever-popular
Pippi Longstocking.

appealing feline personalities in his street and on the sports field, and outwits them with stratagems that are brilliantly realised in comic-book imagery by Stig Lasseby and his colleague Jan Gissberg.

The momentum of Swedish animation has been steadily gathering pace over the past decade. Lasseby's own *Agaton Sax* ("Agaton Sax och Byköpings gästabud", 1976) was screened abroad, and the black-humoured short, *One-armed Bandit,* by Peter Kruuse, has delighted art-house audiences in several countries. According to statistics, no fewer than 75% of present Swedish film animators have started their career during the past fifteen years. There are eight studios in Sweden, and the remaining artists work as free-lancers. The absence of commercial television has denied to these Swedish animators the opportunities for everyday, functional expression that are taken for granted by their colleagues in Britain and the United States. But there is reason now to believe that the pioneering tradition of Victor Bergdahl (whose "Captain Grog" character was developed during the first two decades of the century) will be—literally—re-animated.

Films for children comprise an entire sub-culture in the Nordic countries, and deserve a book to themselves. The Swedish have maintained their place in the vanguard of this development with some exceptional features. Two films of the past eight years serve to illustrate the range of material and expression. *The Brothers Lionheart* ("Bröderna Lejonhjärta", 1977) is an excellent example of the kind of fantasy that can often entrance adults as much as children. Based on a novel by Astrid Lindgren, and made by Olle Hellbom (who until his premature death in 1982 fought for the success of children's films), it evokes medieval virtues and vices in much the same way as *The Seventh Seal* does for adults. There are echoes of Tolkien in *The Brothers Lionheart's* creation of a landscape caught between the forces of good and evil. Lotta Melanton's art direction is outstanding, with painted houses good enough to eat; and the music by Björn Isfält and Lasse Dahlberg sets the mood of other-worldly adventure. The film was screened by the BBC in Britain over several nights, with conspicuous success.

Perhaps the most stimulating aspect of this vogue for children's films has been the obvious willingness on the part of major directors to express their sharpest thoughts in the genre—one need look no further, for example, than Kay Pollak, whose *Elvis! Elvis!* and *Children's Island* have been described above.

In more contemporary a vein, *The Eighth Day* ("Den åttonde dagen", 1978), by Anders Grönroos, deals with the passage from childhood to adolescence, as two shy youngsters meet on holiday and suffer pangs of confusion in the face of their mutual affinities. Grönroos has a cinematic eye akin to Werner Herzog's, with an ability to endow a scene with sudden mystery, and to congeal a moment of fear or wonder in a child's vision.

Thanks to the renown of Astrid Lindgren, some of the more popular Swedish children's films have also been shown outside Scandinavia. As early as 1945, Sandrews produced a version of *Pippi Longstocking* ("Pippi Långstrump"), although the authoress protested in vain at the inclusion of a young loving couple in the film! More than a dozen features have been made subsequently, along with various successful TV series. Other Lindgren characters who have made it to the big screen include boy detective Kalle Blomqvist, Rasmus, Emil, and Karlsson. These harmless entertainments are in sharp contrast to a more portentous "film for children" like *The Big Kids' Party* ("Det stora barnkalaset", 1982), which shows adults behaving like spoiled brats—and thereby flagrantly patronises children as such.

Bergman: the latest phase

Even Ingmar Bergman cocked one eye kindly at the world of children with his marvellous rendition of *The Magic Flute* ("Trollflöjten", 1975), a joyous, zestful homage to Mozart that transcended the bounds of theatrical or operatic experience while never straying too deeply into the dark labyrinth of the soul so often frequented by Bergman.

The past fifteen years have seen Bergman undergo various sea-changes. He purged himself of the gloom that attended his "island" movies of the 1960's, eagerly took up the challenge of the TV mini-

The enchanting Bergman rendition of *The Magic Flute*.

series, plunged into self-imposed exile after a clash with the government tax authorities, and returned in triumph to concoct his crowning glory, *Fanny and Alexander*.

Throughout the period he remained several lengths clear of all other Nordic directors. Many of his works exhibited a welcome eagerness to explore contemporary, rather than metaphysical issues. Although *A Passion* ("En passion", 1969) dealt with spiritual influences, it also included numerous icons of the modern world, and suggested that its eponymous hero, Andreas Winkelmann, was taking refuge on the island of Fårö after committing some crime on the mainland. The farmers and fisherfolk of Fårö attracted Bergman so much that he devoted two full-length documentaries to their lives, and to the injustices he felt they were suffering at the hands of central government. Made ten years apart (1969 and 1979), these eloquent, unpretentious manifestoes were screened on Swedish television.

Gradually, Bergman was coming to grips with the problems of individuals who worked for a livelihood, who drove cars, had apartments in the city, and talked on occasion about money problems. A new generation was able to recognise, if not identify with, the characters in *Scenes from a Marriage*, *The Touch* and *Face to Face*. In all three films, a woman in her thirties stands at the centre of the storm, while the habitually ineffectual Bergman males circle confusedly about her. Bibi Andersson's housewife infatuated with the charms of Elliott Gould's foreign archaeologist in *The Touch* ("Beröringen", 1971) is the most novelettish of these women, but thanks to superlative acting, even she throbs with pain and eagerness. *The Touch*, filmed in English for ABC Pictures Corporation of New York, was underrated at the time of its release; discriminating audiences found it difficult to accept the directness and simplicity of Bergman's dialogue without the convenient filter of subtitles.

Both *Scenes from a Marriage* ("Scener ur ett äktenskap", 1973) and *Face to Face* ("Ansikte mot ansikte", 1976) were made primarily with television in mind. The photography is undistinguished and the emphasis on close-ups inevitably pronounced. The extended format (over 200 minutes) enabled Bergman to develop his relationships in more detail; neither film, however, was the better for being released to cinemas around the world. *Face to Face* contains certain ugly and implausible sequences (the attempted rape, the references to homosexuality) that rob the central element of the film—Jenny's own insecurity despite her profession as psychiatrist—of any emotional impact. Liv Ullmann, intense though she is as Jenny, contributes a more subtle and enduring performance to *Scenes from a Marriage*, which bears a greater stamp of authority than any other Bergman film of the 1970's.

The relationship between Erland Josephson's Johan and Liv Ullmann's Marianne develops along altogether more mature lines than any in Bergman's canon. As husband and wife, they break up, drift towards each other again, and remain, finally, indissolubly bound together and yet leading independent lives. The superficially brittle, but in fact quite resilient façade of a bourgeois marriage is analysed and then swept aside in a sequence of conversations. Dramatic incidents are scarce; Bergman's whole stress is on the way in which words are used to define and defend one's attitudes. In Scandinavia, the film touched a chord among people in many different walks of life. Its approach to women's liberation, to the struggle for precedence between professional and private interests, and to the texture of marital relations in the 1970's, was a revelation to those who had classified Bergman as a religious or mystical director, obsessed with his personal hang-ups.

Erland Josephson, an actor of consummate taste and craftsmanship, has fared less happily as director, although the intelligence of his dialogue is never in question. Both *One and One* ("En och en", 1978) and *The Marmalade Revolution* ("Marmeladupproret", 1980) deal with the difficulties of sustaining relationships in middle age, yet suffer from a lack of humour and a fatal stasis in *mise en scène* (surprising in a stage producer of such experience as Josephson). The failure of these films is all the more galling because of their courage in tackling intellectual dilemmas shunned by the commercial cinema, and because they are both acted and photographed with professional adroitness.

Cries and Whispers ("Viskningar och rop", 1973) summoned up that claustrophobic mood previously associated with Bergman. Set at the turn of the century, in a country mansion clad with scarlet walls and curtains, the film delineates the dying hours of a cancer sufferer (Harriet Andersson), attended by her bickering sisters (Liv Ullmann and Ingrid Thulin) and a faithful maid (Kari Sylwan). Hastening from room to room in anxious silence, united only by their long white dresses, these women constitute a group portrait. Bergman admits that each bears traits of his mother's personality, and he explains the blood-red interiors as having been inspired by a recurring image of the "interior of the soul" as being scarlet and membraneous. Filmed with peerless pictorial style and authority, *Cries and Whispers* is as much a tribute to the art of cinematographer Sven Nykvist as to Bergman himself, and the ensemble acting of the four women ranks with the work of Eva Dahlbeck, Ingrid Thulin, and Bibi Andersson in *So Close to Life.*

In January, 1976, Bergman was arrested by the tax police while rehearsing at the Royal Dramatic Theatre in Stockholm. Disconcerted and profoundly shaken by the experience of the next few weeks, he decided to quit his native country, and in April took up residence in Munich. The case against him and his production company was dismissed and the officials involved were reprimanded, but Bergman's work was scarred by the humiliation. The three features he completed "in exile", *The Serpent's Egg, Autumn Sonata,* and *From the Life of the Marionettes,* contain dark currents of anguish and misanthropy that impede their flow.

The Serpent's Egg was made in 1976 for the Italian producer Dino De Laurentiis, in co-production with a German company. In it, Bergman sought to recreate the spirit of that turbulent week in November, 1923, when the value of the Deutschmark tumbled to virtually nothing, and Fascism was beginning to emerge from its fragile shell. Perhaps in the end there were too many hurdles for Bergman to surmount: the difficulty of shooting in a foreign country for the first time; the presence of a Hollywood star (David Carradine) in the lead; a budget that exceeded $3 million and entailed the construction of a vast set at the Bavaria Studios outside Munich; the marshalling of some 3,000 extras; and a narrative that fused elements of stark realism and nightmarish horror. Here Bergman's human characters are mere marionettes, twisting and writing in the grip of an unseen cosmic destiny. *The Serpent's Egg* does not work as a police thriller, but its images of corruption and cruelty spring full-bloodedly from the screen, in contrast to the cloying sweetness of *Cabaret,* which deals more frivolously with a similar period and theme.

Autumn Sonata (1977), filmed in Norway with financial backing from Britain's Lew Grade, brought together two of Scandinavia's finest actresses, Ingrid Bergman and Liv Ullmann. As mother and daughter,

Two famous Scandinavian faces, Ingrid Bergman and Liv Ullmann together with Halvar Björk in *Autumn Sonata*.

they spend a couple of days in moral and psychological battle. Liv Ullmann's Eva is a mouse-like parson's wife, living with her handicapped sister in a remote country vicarage. Her mother, a renowned concert pianist, arrives with effusive comments about her travels and triumphs, conveniently neglecting to confront the presence in the house of her younger daughter who, it transpires, has been sacrificed on the altar of her mother's career. The command of dialogue exchange is remarkable, as always in Bergman, and *Autumn Sonata* profits from an intimacy and economy of expression that recalls *Scenes from a Marriage*. The scene in which Ingrid Bergman and Liv Ullmann play a

Chopin Prelude, with each chord aquiver with suppressed emotion, belongs to any anthology of Bergman's work.

Returning to Munich, Bergman embarked on a bitter *voyage au bout de la nuit*. Nothing about *From the Life of the Marionettes* is harmonious. The playing is flat and theatrical, the monochrome photography by the normally immaculate Nykvist looks muddy and uninspired, and the dialogue sounds rhetorical and under-rehearsed. The sense of an artist close to spinning off into insanity pervades the film, and despite its story of marital crisis unfolding in contemporary Munich, this harsh groan of protest evokes the stifling conflicts of Bergman's 1940's works.

When *Fanny and Alexander* ("Fanny och Alexander", 1982) was announced as being Bergman's final film for the cinema, few admirers could have believed that it would emerge as one of the master's most enjoyable and relaxed films, a long exquisite tapestry of a movie that earned respectable sums at the box-office in Scandinavia and the US, as well as a cluster of awards. *Fanny and Alexander* pays affectionate tribute to Bergman's recollections of childhood. Set in 1907—admittedly some 15 years before Bergman could have recalled such an atmosphere—it traces the joys and sorrows of a mighty family in the town of Uppsala. Those stalwart pillars of Bergman's world, Church and Theatre, collide in headlong opposition, the one representing dignity and repression, the other hedonism and generosity. The opening sequence, observing the Ekdahls celebrating Christmas, occupies almost an hour in the TV version of the film, and scarcely seems a minute too long. Nor would one wish any abridgement of the scenes in the Bishop's mansion, where the children Fanny and Alexander are incarcerated against their will. Bergman's "Gobelin", as he likes to call it, contains innumerable figures and fancies from which one may choose the ones that fascinate the most. None, it must be said, is scrutinised in great depth; *Fanny and Alexander* is more an attempt to recapture a specific time and place. Bergman's team excels itself in terms of costumes, sets, lighting, sound, and makeup. Every composition boasts a sumptuous depth and texture. The TV version, running a good 100 minutes longer than the three-hour theatrical print, proceeds along a smoother narra-

141

Gun Wållgren and Erland Josephson rest after the rigours of Yuletide celebrations in *Fanny and Alexander*.

tive line, and cherishes in reserve several scenes denied to the cinema patron (for example, an extraordinary dream vision with wailing penitents, Harriet Andersson flaunting her stigmata, and Death with his scythe reminiscent of *The Seventh Seal*).

Most critics agree that Bergman could not have concluded his career as a film-maker on a higher note. Yet, like many a great athlete and public entertainer, Bergman's retirement is premature. He still teems with ideas for work on television, big screen, and the stage. Besides, Swedish cinema needs him in a period when all too few domestic films are exerting either influence or appeal on world markets. Bergman is both the envy and the inspiration of Swedish directors. They may resent working in his shadow, but they also bask in the light of his achievement and celebrity. For many artists and critics around the world, he is quite simply the greatest of all film directors. Bergman himself would be the first to acknowledge the enormous contribution made by his players and technicians, who together continue a tradition stretching back to 1912, when Sjöström and Stiller first persuaded Swedish audiences that film could—and would—be an art.

Bergman will probably never retire—he has made a TV film, *After the Rehearsal* ("Efter repetitionen", 1983), which was released abroad as a theatrical feature and received glowing reviews in the United States; and he has announced his desire to make a screen version of Astrid Lindgren's *Lotta på Bråkmakargatan,* a children's book. "It would be a nice way to spend a summer," he declared in early 1984.

Today—and tomorrow?

During the course of the last decade the pattern of Swedish production has to an increasing extent been forced to bow to the pressures and realities of the modern box-office. Ambitious productions, such as Troell's *The Flight of the Eagle,* require considerable investment from abroad. TV rights are vital; so too—where the really big films are concerned—is the mini-series format that has enabled both *The Flight of the Eagle* and *Fanny and Alexander* to be aired on the small screen over a period of weeks. The influence of television may also be responsible for the gathering tide of documentaries, covering everything from rock music (from ABBA to EBBA) to nuclear power *(The Last Warning,* "Sista varningen"), ecology *(Nature's Revenge),* to death by cancer *(Courage to Live,* "Mod att leva"). The activity of such organisations as FilmCentrum, Folkets Bio, which releases socially-conscious films, and Föreningsfilmo, proves that there is a need—and, to some extent, a demand—for statements that address an audience through the traditional medium of film but that may be used to start discussion and debate as much as to entertain a weekend audience. Stefan Jarl's *Nature's Revenge* ("Naturens hämnd", 1983) has dramatically

Selected for screening at the New York Film Festival in 1984, *A Hill on the Dark Side of the Moon* ("Berget på månens baksida") dealt with the problems of female emancipation in the 1880's, and resulted from a close collaboration between writer Agneta Pleijel and director Lennart Hjulström. Here: Gunilla Nyros as Sonya Kovalevsky.

enhanced the reputation of such documentaries. Photographed with awesome skill and sensitivity by Per Källberg, it sets up a vibrant dialectic between the lyrical bounty of Swedish landscape and the threat from chemical fertilisers and toxic sprays. Wildlife and flora are equally at risk. Interspersing its evocative shots of lakes and forests are comments from conservationists who actually have to cope with the damage inflicted by man-made chemicals.

Agneta Elers-Jarleman and Jean Montgrenier in *Beyond Sorrow, Beyond Pain.*

Beyond Sorrow, Beyond Pain ("Smärtgränsen", 1983), directed by Agneta Elers-Jarleman, is equally courageous—but on an acutely personal level. The director's beloved life companion was suddenly injured in a street accident so badly that it seems unlikely he will ever again function as a normal human being. The documentary recaptures the agony of this shock, and the acceptance of a new reality, fuelled by a resolve that the circumstances must never be allowed to overwhelm the human spirit.

Swedish cinema has, perhaps, not enjoyed in the final analysis quite the easiest of rides. In 1984, Svensk Filmindustri and Europa Film were

Ronja, The Robber's Daughter, the latest in a long line of distinguished and entertaining children's films that also appeal to an adult audience. Here: Hanna Zetterberg, Börje Ahlstedt and Lena Nyman.

forced to merge in order to ensure survival (Europa was in severe difficulties), and this in turn has meant that while the Film Institute can offer production guarantees to film-makers, it cannot so easily find co-producers from the private sector. Despite this handicap, the prospects are still quite bright, with Mai Zetterling returning to Sweden to shoot a new film in 1984/85, and the Soviet exile, Andrei Tarkovsky, also signed to make a picture in Sweden starring Erland Josephson.

The triumph of *Fanny and Alexander* at the Academy Awards has given fresh impetus to all those at work in Swedish film. The national economy may be in poor shape, but the will to express feelings on film can transcend such temporary difficulties providing the infra-structure is solid, and with the Swedish Film Institute determined to support new talent, there is every prospect that some new Troell, Widerberg, or even Bergman, will arise before the decade's end.

Index of Films Cited in the Text

Original Swedish titles in alphabetical order

Figures in bold type indicate more detailed references

Agaton Sax och Byköpings gästabud, 1976 *(Agaton Sax)* 134
Andra dansen, 1983 *(The Second Dance)* **124—125**
Ansikte mot ansikte, 1976 *(Face to Face)* **137**
Ansiktet, 1958 *(The Face/The Magician)* 52, **56**
Att angöra en brygga, 1965 *(Go Ashore)* 117
Att älska, 1964 *(To Love)* **73**
Autumn Sonata, 1977 *(Höstsonaten)* 84, **139—141**
Avskedet, 1983 *(The Farewell)* **125**

Baltutlämningen, 1970 *(A Baltic Tragedy)* **111**
Bang!, 1977 *(Bang!)* 129
Banketten, 1948 *(The Banquet)* 32
Bara en mor, 1949 *(Only a Mother)* 35, **36**, 50
Barabbas, 1952 *(Barabbas)* **49**
Barnförbjudet, 1980 *(Elephant Walk)* **123**
Barnens ö, 1980 (Children's Island) **123**, 124, 135
Barnvagnen, 1962 *(The Baby Carriage/The Pram)* 67, 69, **70**
Berg-Ejvind och hans hustru, 1917 *(The Outlaw and His Wife)* **11—13**, 25
Berget på månens baksida, 1983 *(A Hill on the Dark Side of the Moon)* **144**
Beröringen, 1971 *(The Touch)* **137**
Brusten himmel, 1982 *(Broken Sky)* **112**
Bröderna Lejonhjärta, 1977 *(The Brothers Lionheart)* 132, **134**

De svarta maskerna, 1912 *(The Black Masks)* **16**
Den allvarsamma leken, 1977 *(Games of Love and Loneliness)* **111**
Den enarmade banditen, 1973 *(One-armed Bandit)* 134
Den enfaldige mördaren, 1982 *(The Simple-Minded Murderer)* **118**, 119, 121

Den magiska cirkeln, 1970 *(Beyond the Line of Duty)* **111—112**

Den starkaste, 1929 *(The Strongest)* **24—25**, 28

Den vita sporten, 1968 *(The White Game)* 95, **96—97**

Den vita väggen, 1975 *(The White Wall)* **110**

Den åttonde dagen, 1978 *(The Eighth Day)* **135**

Deserter USA, 1969 **87**

Det brinner en eld, 1943 *(There Burned a Flame)* **27**

Det omringade huset, 1922 *(The Surrounded House)* 23

Det regnar på vår kärlek, 1946 *(Its Rains on Our Love/Man with an Umbrella)* 38

Det sista äventyret, 1974 *(The Last Adventure)* **125—126**

Det sjunde inseglet, 1956 *(The Seventh Seal)* 12, 51, **52—53**, 118, 134, 142

Det stora barnkalaset, 1982 *(The Big Kid's Party)* **135**

Det stora äventyret, 1953 *(The Great Adventure)* **62**, 63

Djävulens öga, 1960 *(The Devil's Eye)* **59**, 115

Domaren, 1960 *(The Judge)* 64

Dom kallar oss mods, 1968 *(They Call Us Misfits)* **93**

Dunderklumpen, 1974 130

Efter repetitionen, 1983 *(After the Rehearsal)* **143**

Elvira Madigan, 1967 68, 69, 70, **71—73**, 99, 113

Elvis! Elvis!, 1976 **123**, 135

En djungelsaga, 1957 *(The Flute and the Arrow)* **62**

En och en, 1978 *(One and One)* **138**

En dröm om frihet, 1969 *(A Dream of Freedom)* **90**

En handfull kärlek, 1974 *(A Handful of Love)* **112—113**

En kille och en tjej, 1975 *(Boy Meets Girl)* 115

En kluven värld, 1948 *(A Divided World)* **30—32**

En kärlekshistoria, 1970 *(A Swedish Love Story)* **120**, 121

En kärlekssommar, 1979 *(A Summer's Love)* **116**

En lektion i kärlek, 1954 *(A Lesson in Love)* 46, **50**

En natt, 1931 *(One Night)* **25**

En passion, 1969 *(A Passion/The Passion of Anna)* 136

En söndag i september, 1963 *(A Sunday in September)* 67, **73**
En vandring i solen, 1979 *(Walking in the Sun)* **116**
Erotikon, 1920 **17—18**
Ett anständigt liv, 1979 *(A Respectable Life)* **93—94**
Ett brott, 1940 *(A Crime)* **28**
Eva, 1948 27

Fanny och Alexander, 1982 *(Fanny and Alexander)* 136, **141—143**, 146
Flicka och hyacinter, 1950 *(Girls with Hyacinths)* **33**, 34
Frihetens murar, 1979 *(Roots of Grief)* **122**
From the Life of the Marionettes, 1978 *(Ur marionetternas liv/Aus dem Leben der Marionetten)* 139, **141**
Frånskild, 1951 *(Divorced)* 27
Främmande hamn, 1948 *(Foreign Harbour)* **29**
Fröken Julie, 1950 *(Miss Julie)* 43, **44—45**, 46, 47, 50, 55, 79
491, 1964 67, **90—91**
Fängelse, 1948 *(Prison/The Devil's Wanton)* **40—41**
För att inte tala om alla dessa kvinnor, 1964 *(All These Women/Now About These Women)* 17, 115
Första divisionen, 1941 *(First Division)* **32**
Förvandlingen, 1976 *(Metamorphosis)* **126—127**

Giftas, 1956 *(Married)* **55**
Giliap, 1976 **120—121**
Gubben kommer, 1939 *(The Old Man's Coming)* 37
Gud fader och tattaren, 1954 *(God and the Gipsyman)* **29**
Gunnar Hedes saga, 1922 *(Gunnar Hedes Saga/The Old Mansion)* **21**
Gycklarnas afton, 1953 *(Sawdust and Tinsel/The Naked Night)* 32, 46, **47—48**
Gösta Berlings saga, 1924 *(The Atonement of Gösta Berling/Gösta Berlings Saga)* **21**

Hallo Baby, 1976 **123**
Hamnstad, 1948 *(Port of Call)* **39—40**, 50

Harry Munter, 1969 100, **103−104**
Hempas bar, 1976 *(Triumph Tiger '57)* **114−115**
Hemåt i natten, 1977 *(Homeward in the Night)* **110**
Hemsöborna, 1955 *(The People of Hemsö)* **61**
Herr Arnes penningar, 1919 *(Sir Arne's Treasure/The Treasure of Arne)*
    8, 18, **19**, **21**
Hets, 1944 *(Frenzy/Torment)* 36, 38, **39**, 50
Himlaspelet, 1942 *(The Road to Heaven)* 27, **34−36**, 50, 118
Hon dansade en sommar, 1951 *(One Summer of Happiness)* 60, **61**
Hugo och Josefin, 1967 *(Hugo and Josephine)* 99, **102−103**
Hägringen, 1959 *(Mirage)* **59**
Här har du ditt liv, 1966 *(Here Is Your Life)* 80, **81−82**, 83, 119
Höstsonaten, see *Autumn Sonata*

Ingeborg Holm, 1913 *(Ingeborg Holm/Give Us This Day)* **9−10**, 12, 24
Ingenjör Andrées luftfärd, 1982 *(The Flight of the Eagle)* **130,** 131, 143
Ingmarssönerna, 1918 *(The Sons of Ingmar)* **14**
Intermezzo, 1936 25, **26−27**, 116
Iris och löjtnantshjärta, 1946 *(Iris and the Lieutenant)* 28, **36**

Jag – en kvinna, 1965 *(I−a Woman)* **79−80**
Jag heter Stelios, 1977 *(Foreigners)* **110−111**
Jag är med barn, 1979 *(Father To Be)* **115**
Jag är nyfiken – blå, 1968 *(I am Curious−Blue),* **76−77**, 80
Jag är nyfiken – gul, 1967 *(I am Curious−Yellow)* 61, 68, 69, **76**, 77, 80
Jakob – smitaren, 1983 *(Where Were You Jacob?)* **123**
Johan, 1921 **18−19**
Jungfrukällan, 1960 *(The Virgin Spring)* 19, **56−59**, 75
Juninatten, 1940 *(June Night)* 37
Jönssonligan får guldfeber, 1984 (prelim. title *The Jonsson Gang*
    Catches Gold-fever) 116
Jönssonligan och Dynamit-Harry, 1982 *(The Jonsson Gang Meets Dy-*
    namite-Harry) 116

Karin Ingmarsdotter, 1920 *(Karin, Daughter of Ingmar)* **14**

Karin Månsdotter, 1954 **49**

Kattorna, 1965 *(The Cats)* 77

Kejsaren, 1979 *(The Emperor)* **121**

Klänningen, 1964 *(The Dress)* **75**

Korridoren, 1968 *(The Corridor)* **90**

Kris, 1945 *(Crisis)* 38

Kristoffers hus, 1980 *(Christopher's House)* **122**

Kungajakt, 1943 *(The Royal Hunt)* 27, **33—34**

Kvarteret Korpen, 1963 *(Raven's End)* **80—81**

Kvinnodröm, 1955 *(Journey into Autumn/Dreams)* 46, **47**, 48

Kvinna utan ansikte, 1947 *(Woman without a Face)* 27

Kvinnors väntan, 1952 *(Waiting Women/Secrets of Women)* 46, 50

Käre John, 1964 *(Dear John)* **69**

Kärlek och journalistik, 1916 *(Love and Journalism)* **16**, 17

Kärlek och kassabrist, 1932 *(Love and Deficit)* 24

Kärlek och landstorm, 1931 *(Love and the Home Guard)* 24

Kärleken segrar, 1916 *(The Victory of Love)* **8**

Kärlek 65 *(Love 65)* 69, **70—71**

Kärlekens bröd, 1953 *(The Bread of Love)* **61**

Kärlekens språk *(The Language of Love)* **80**

Körkarlen, 1921 *(Thy Soul Shall Bear Witness/The Phantom Carriage/ The Phantom Chariot)* 13, **14—15**

Limpan, 1983 *(Loafie)* **119—120**

Linus, 1979 **112**

Livet är stenkul, 1967 *(Life's Just Great)* 90

Lotta på Bråkmakargatan 143

Luftburen, 1972 *(The Air Cage)* **126**

Lyckliga skitar, 1970 *(Blushing Charlie)* **112**

Lyftet, 1978 *(The Score)* **127—128**

Långt borta och nära, 1977 *(Near and Far Away* **121—122**

Made in Sweden, 1969 **97—98**

Mamma, 1983 *(Our Life Is Now)* **113—114**

Mannen från Mallorca, 1984 *(The Man from Mallorca)* 129
Mannen på taket, 1976 *(The Man on the Roof)* **128**
Mannen som blev miljonär, 1980 *(To Be a Millionaire)* **116**
Mannen som slutade röka, 1972 *(The Man Who Gave Up Smoking)*
117—118
Maria, 1975 **128**
Marmeladupproret, 1980 *(The Marmalade Revolution)* **138**
Med livet som insats, 1939 *(They Staked Their Lives)* **28**
Mina drömmars stad, 1977 *(City of My Dreams)* **111**
Misshandlingen, 1969 *(The Assault/Assault)* **91—92**, 122
Mitt hem är Copacabana, 1965 *(My Home Is Copacabana)* **62**, **98—99**
Mod att leva, 1983 *(Courage to Live)* 143
Musik i mörker, 1947 *(Music in Darkness/Night Is My Future)* 38
Myglaren, 1966 *(The Grafter)* **92—93**
Mysteriet natten till den 25:e, 1916 *(The Mystery of the Night of the 24th)* **8**
Målaren, 1982 *(The Painter)* **123**
Måndagarna med Fanny, 1977 *(Robert and Fanny)* **122**
Människor i stad, 1947 *(Rhythm of a City)* **30**
Mästerman, 1920 *(Master Man)* 23

Natt i hamn, 1943 *(Night in the Harbour)* **29—30**
Nattlek, 1966 *(Night Games)* 77, **79**
Nattvardsgästerna, 1963 *(Winter Light/The Communicants)* 64, 84, **85**,
87
Naturens hämnd, 1983 *(Nature's Revenge)* 107, **108**, **143—144**
Ni ljuger, 1969 *(You're Lying)* **91**
Norrtullsligan, 1923 *(The Norrtull Gang)* 37
Nybyggarna, 1972 *(The New Land)* **105**, 129
Nära livet, 1958 *(So Close to Life/Brink of Life)* **55—56**, 139
När ängarna blommar, 1946 *(When Meadows Bloom)* **29**

Ola & Julia, 1967 90
Ole dole doff, 1968 *(Who Saw Him Die?/Eeny Meeny Miney Moe)*
82—84

Om sju flickor, 1974 *(Sevens Girls)* **108**
Ombyte av tåg, 1943 *(Changing Trains)* **32**
Ormens ägg, see *The Serpent's Egg*

Paradistorg, 1976 *(Paradise Place/Summer Paradise)* **108**
P+B, 1984 **118**
Pelle Svanslös, 1981 *(Peter-No-Tail)* **132—134**
Persona, 1966 **85—87**, 88
Pettersson + Bendel, 1933 28
Picassos äventyr, 1978 *(The Adventures of Picasso)* 118
Pionjärerna, see *Zandy's Bride*
Pippi Långstrump, *(Pippi Longstocking)* 133, **135**
Pistolen, 1973 *(The Pistol)* **127**
Pojken i trädet, 1961 *(The Boy in the Tree)* 62
Pojken och draken, 1961 *(The Boy and the Kite)* **69**
Puss och kram, 1967 *(Hugs and Kisses)* 99, **100—101**

Repmånad, 1978 *(The Call-up)* **115**
Rid i natt!, 1942 *(Ride Tonight!)* **27**, 37
Riten, 1969 *(The Rite/The Ritual!)* **89**
Ronja Rövardotter, 1984 *(Ronja, The Robber's Daughter)* 146

Salka Valka, 1954 **61**
Sally och friheten, 1981 *(Sally and Freedom)* **108—109**
Scener ur ett äktenskap, 1973 *(Scenes from a Marriage)* **137—138**, 140
Sista varningen, 1980 *(The Last Warning)* **143—144**
Skammen, 1968 *(Shame/The Shame)* **87—89**
Skepp till Indialand, 1947 *(A Ship Bound for India/Land of Desire)* 38
Skärseld, 1974 *(Purgatorio)* **126**
Slumrande toner, 1977 *(For Your Pleasure)* **110**
Släpp fångarne loss – det är vår, 1976 *(Let the Prisoners Go, for It's Spring)* 118
Smultronstället, 1957 *(Wild Strawberries)* 53, 54, **55**
Smärtgränsen, 1983 *(Beyond Sorrow, Beyond Pain)* **145**

... som havets nakna vind, 1968 *(As the Naked Wind from the Sea)* 61
Som natt och dag, 1969 *(Like Night and Day)* 99, **101–102**
Sommaren med Monika, 1952 *(Summer with Monika/Monika)* 45,
    46–47
Sommarlek, 1951 *(Summer Interlude/Illicit Interlude)* 42, **43–44**, 53
Sommarnattens leende, 1955 *(Smiles of a Summer Night)* 17, **50–52**,
    53, 61, 115
Sopor, 1981 *(Refuse)* 118
Svenska Bilder, 1964 *(Swedish Pictures)* 117
Sven Klangs kvintett, 1977 *(Sven Klang's Combo)* 105, **114**
Swedenhielms, 1935 **25–26**
Syskonbädd 1782, 1966 *(My Sister My Love)* **75–76**
Såsom i en spegel, 1961 *(Through a Glass Darkly)* 64, **84**, 85, 86, 87
Sällskapsresan, 1980 *(The Charter Trip)* **115**
Söderkåkar, 1932 *(The Southsiders)* 24

Terje Vigen, 1916 *(A Man There Was)* **11**, 12
The Serpent's Egg, 1976 *(Ormens ägg/Das Schlangenei)* **139**
Thomas Graals bästa barn, 1918 *(Thomas Graal's First Child)* **17**
Thomas Graals bästa film, 1917 *(Thomas Graal's Best Film)* **17**
Till glädje, 1950 *(To Joy)* **42–43**, 44
Trollflöjten, 1975 *(The Magic Flute)* 87, 135, 136
Trut!, 1944 *(The Gull/Sea Hawk)* **30**
Trädgårdsmästaren, 1912 *(The Gardener/The Broken Spring Rose)* **9**
Två killar och en tjej, 1983 *(Happy We)* **115**
Tystnaden, 1963 *(The Silence)* 64, 69, **84–85**, 86, 108
Törst, 1949 *(Thirst/Three Strange Loves)* **40**, **41–42**
Tösen från Stormyrtorpet, 1917 *(The Girl from the Marsh Croft)* **11–12**

Ubåt 39, 1952 **30**
Uppdraget, 1977 *(The Assignment)* **128**
Utvandrarna, 1971 *(The Emigrants)* **105**, 106, 111, 119, 129
Ur marionetternas liv, see *From the Life of the Marionettes*

Vargtimmen, 1968 *(Hour of the Wolf)* **87, 155**
Varning för Jönssonligan, 1981 *(Beware of the Jonsson Gang)* **116**
Vildfåglar, 1955 *(Wild Birds)* **50**
Viskningar och rop, 1973 *(Cries and Whispers)* **138—139**
Värmlänningarna, 1909 *(The People of Värmland)* **6**

Zandy's Bride, 1974 *(Pionjärerna)* 129

Ådalen 31, 1969 *(The Ådalen Riots)* 24, **99**, 112
Åke och hans värld, 1984 *(Åke and His World)* **120**

Ägget är löst!, 1974 *(Egg, Egg, A Hardboiled Story)* 118
Älskande par, 1964 *(Loving Couples)* **77—79**
Älskarinnan, 1962 *(The Mistress)* 67, **73—75**
Änglar, finns dom?, 1961 *(Do You Believe in Angels?)* 79
Äppelkriget, 1971 *(The Apple War)* 117

Index of Names Cited in the Text

Figures in bold type indicate more detailed references

Agosto, Silvano 126
Ahlstedt, Börje 146
Ahrne, Marianne 120, 122
Alfredson, Hans 28, **116–118**
Andersson, Bibi 53, 54, 59, 73, 74, 75, 88, 137, 139
Andersson, Harriet 47, 48, 73, 110, 114, 138, 142
Andersson, Olof 23
Andersson, Roy 120, 121
Andrée, S. A. 130
Anschütz, Ottomar 5
Antonioni, Michelangelo 71, 124
Arehn, Mats 116, **128**
Axberg, Eddie 82, 83

Bach, Johann Sebastian 30
Bán, Frigyes 29
Bandler, Vivica 125
Barrie, J. M. 99
Beck, Lili 9
Bergdahl, Victor 134
Bergenstråhle, Johan 68, 97–98, **110–111**, 123
Berggren, Thommy 70, 71, 81, 120, 122
Berglund, Per 111
Bergman, Ingmar 12, 17,
19, 22, 27, 29, 30, 32, 33, 34, **37–44**, 45, **46–49**, **50–59**, 62, 64, 65, 66, 69, 79, **84–89**, 93, **108**, 110, 115, 125, **135–143**, 146
Bergman, Ingrid 24, 26–27, 84, 116, **139–140**
Björk, Anita 45, 46, 55
Björk, Halvar 140
Björkman, Stig 110
Björnstrand, Gunnar 47, 51, 52, 89
Branner, Per-Axel 28
Breien, Anja 111
Brost, Gudrun 56
Broström, Gunnel 55, 61
Brömssen, Tomas von 129
Buñuel, Louis 79, 89, 101

Carlsen, Henning 77
Carné, Marcel 15, 33
Carradine, David 139
Cassavetes, John 70
Chopin, Frédéric 141
Chorell, Walentin 78
Christensson, Irma 116
Claesson, Stig 116
Cornell, Jonas 68, 99, **100–102**, 116
Costa-Gavras, Constantin 90
Curtiz, Michael 32
Cybulski, Zbigniew 73

Dagerman, Stig 37
Dahl, Christer 127
Dahlbeck, Eva 35, 36, 51, 52, 78, 139
Dahlberg, Erik 6
Dahlberg, Hans, 108, 116
Dahlberg, Lasse 134
Danielsson, Tage **117–118**
Dante, Alighieri 126
De Geer Bergenstråhle, Marie-Louise 120, **123**
Degermark, Pia 70, 71
Dittmar, Ernst 6
Doinel, Antoine 115
Donne, John 126
Donner, Jörn 67, **73**
Donskoi, Mark 28
Dreyer, Carl 14
Dvořák, Ivo 126
Dymling, Carl Anders 30, 47, 52, 64, 67

Edlund, Bibi 116
Edwall, Allan 56, **118–120**
Eisenstein, Sergei 21
Ejve, Ingemar, 116
Ek, Anders 89
Ek, Malin 113, 114
Ekerot, Bengt 51

Ekman, Carl G. 24
Ekman, Gösta, Sr.
 25−27, 32, 116
Ekman, Gösta, Jr.
 32, 115, **116−118**
Ekman, Hasse 28, **32**,
 40, 116
Ekman, Mikael 116
Ekmanner, Agneta 100,
 101
Elers-Jarleman, Agneta
 145
Ellington, Duke 99
Engdahl, Carl 6
von Essen, Siri 44
Evander, Per Gunnar
 125

Faustman, Hampe
 28−30
Fellini, Federico 70
Feuillade, Louis 8
FilmCentrum **94−96**, 143
Fischer, Gunnar 6, 30,
 53, 57
Florman, Ernest 5
Fogelström, Per-Anders
 111
Folkets Bio 96, 143
Forsberg, Lasse **91**, **122**
Forslund, Bengt 82, 126
Forssell, Lars 89
Fridell, Åke 45, 53
Frost, David 115
Fröling, Ewa 108, 109
Föreningsfilmo 143

Garbo, Greta 15, 16, 20,
 21, 22, 23
Gillett, John 14
Gissberg, Jan 134
Godard, Jean-Luc 70

Gould, Elliott 137
Grade, Lew 139
Granhagen, Lena 97
Grede, Kjell 99,
 102−104
Grevenius, Herbert 37
Gripe, Maria 103, 123
Grönberg, Åke 48
Grönroos, Anders 135
Guinness, Alec 53
Gustafsson, Björn 116
Görling, Lars 90

Hagelbäck, Jösta 120,
 121
Halldoff, Jan 68, **90**,
 115, **125−126**
Hallström, Lasse 115
Hammarén, Torsten 37
Hanson, Lars 21
Hansson, Per Albin 28
Hassner, Rune 92, 93
Hasso, Signe 24
Heiknert, Carl-Axel 125
Hell, Erik 89
Hellbom, Olle 134
Henning, Eva 33, 42
Henrikson, Anders 28,
 45, 55
Herzog, Werner 135
Hitchcock, Alfred 125
Hjelm, Keve 70, 81
Hjulström, Lennart 144
Hoffman, Dustin 128
Hoffman, E.T.A. 87
Holmberg, Henric 114
Holmberg, Sten 121

Ibsen, Henrik 10, 11, 55
Idestam-Almquist, Bengt
 17, 41

Isaksson, Ulla 75
Isfält, Björn 134
Iveberg, Hans 115

Jacobsson, Ulla 52, 61
Jaenzon, Julius 6, 7, 14,
 19
Jarl, Stefan **93−94**,
 95, 107, 108, 120,
 143−144
Jersild, P. C. 123, 124
Johnson, Eyvind 82
Johnson, Mary 8, 18,
 19, 21
Josephson, Erland 120,
 137, **138**, 142, 146
Jung, C. G. 86
Järrel, Stig 39

Kafka, Franz 126
Keaton, Buster 24, 99
Kjellin, Alf 36
Klercker, Georg 7, 8
Knutsson, Gösta 132
Kreuger, Ivar 23, 24, 28
Krook, Margaretha 45
Krusenstjerna, Agnes
 78
Kruuse, Peter 134
Kulle, Jarl 49, 51, 69
Kurosawa, Akira 59
Käll, Susanna 112
Källberg, Per 144

Lagerkvist, Pär 49
Lagerlöf, Selma 14, 19,
 21, 34
Lambert, Lars 87
Landgré, Inga 53
Laretei, Käbi 59
Lasseby, Stig **132−134**

De Laurentiis, Dino 139
Laxness, Halldór 61
Lean, David 15
Lidman, Sara 89
Lindberg, Per 37
Lindblom, Gunnel 53,
  56, 86, **108—109**
Lindegren, Erik 37
Lindgren, Astrid 103,
  119, 134, **135**, 143
Lindgren, Lars-Magnus
  69, 79
Lindgren, Peter 111
Lindman, Arvid 24
Lindquist, Jan 93, 95
Lindström, Jon 110
Lindström, Rune 34
Ljungberger, Erik 8,
Loach, Kenneth 108
Lubitsch, Ernst 17
Lundgren, P. A. 53, 113
Länsberg, Olle 69
Lönnbro, Anders 128

Magnusson, Charles 5, 6,
  7, 9, 11, 14, 23, 67
Mailer, Norman 76
Malmer, Lennart 96
Malmsjö, Jan 8
Malmsten, Birger 29, 38,
  40, 41
Marmstedt, Lorens 40
Marx, Karl 82
Mattsson, Arne 60,
  61, 68
Maugham, Somerset 50
Mayer, Louis B. 49
Melanton, Lotta 134
Meschke, Michael 126
Moberg, Vilhelm 27,
  37, 105

Molander, Gustaf
  25—27, 37
Molander, Karin 17
Montgrenier, Jean 145
Mozart, Wolfgang
  Amadeus 72, 135
Myrberg, Per 74, 97
Myrdal, Alva 92
Myrdal, Gunnar 92
Myrdal, Jan 92, 93

Nielsen, Jan 103, 104
Nilsson, Erik M. 94, 95
Nilsson, Göran 125
Nilsson, Maj-Britt 42
Niskanen, Tuija-Maija
  125
Nordgren, Erik 53
Nykvist, Sven 56—57, 58,
  85, 139, 141
Nylander, Nils Hanson 6
Nyman, Lena 76, 90

Ohlson, Robert 6
O'Konor, Louise 95
Oktober 114
Olin, Stig 38, 42, 44
Olofson, Christina 120,
  123
Olsson, Ninne 114
Olsson, Stellan 114
Óskarsson, Lárus 120,
  124—125
Östen, Suzanne 113—114

Palme, Olof 77
Palme, Ulf 45, 49
Persson, Edvard 24
Persson, Essy 79
Persson, Jörgen 96, 113
Persson, Kent 114

Petersen, Knut 91, 92
Pehrsson, Jan 125
Pinter, Harold
Pleijel, Agneta 144
Plummer, Christopher
  128
Polanski, Roman 124
Pollak, Kay 120, **123**,
  124, 135
Poppe, Nils 53
Presley, Elvis 114

Ragnar, Per 90
Reed, Carol 15
du Rées, Göran 120, **123**
Reinhardt, Max 37
Renoir, Jean 8, 15
Resnais, Alain 61, 102
Rhudin, Fridolf 24
Romare, Ingela 96
Rosi, Francesco 90
Ruud, Sif 108, 116

Sandrew, Anders 67
Scarlatti, Domenico 59
Schein, Harry **66**, 67, 105
Schollin, Christina, 69
Scott, Robert Falcon 130
Seth, Carl Johan 108
Sjöberg, Alf 22, 24—25,
  27, 28, **32—36**, 37,
  39, **43—46**, 47, **49—50**,
  55, 59, 62, 64, 68, 79,
  84
Sjögren, Olle 87
Sjöman, Vilgot 67, 68,
  69, 70, **73—77**, **90—91**,
  108, 112
Sjöström, Victor 5, 6,
  8—15, 16, 17, 19, 21,

22, 23, 25, 30, 34, 43, 50, 53, 54, 55, 82, 143
Sjöwall, Maj 128
Skarsgård, Stellan 118, 119
Skogsberg, Ingvar 111
Stangertz, Göran 126
Stiller, Mauritz 5, 6, 8, 9, **15—22**, 23, 25, 50, 73, 143
Stridbeck, Moa 113
Strindberg, August 44, 55, 61
Strömstedt, Lasse 127—128
Sucksdorff, Arne **30—32**, **62**, 68, **98**
Sundman, Per Olof 130
Sundström, Frank 78
Svedlund, Doris 41
Svenstedt, Carl Henrik 95
Sydow, Max von 45, 51, 53, 56, 73, 88, 98, 130
Sylwan, Kari 138
Söderberg, Hjalmar 111

Tarkovsky, Andrei 146

Tati, Jacques 115
Taube, Inger 70
Teje, Tora 17
Tengroth, Birgit 33, 41, 42
Thelestam, Lars 114—115
Thulin, Ingrid 86, 89, **112**, 138, 139
Tidblad, Inga 127
Tirl, Jiří 127
Tissé, Eduard 21
Tolkien, J. R. R. 134
Tracy, Spencer 49
Troell, Jan 22, 68, 69, 80, **82—84**, 105, **129—130**, 131, 143, 146
Truffaut, François 70, 115
Törnblom, Stig 83

Ullmann, Liv 87, 88, 137, 138, **139—140**

Valberg, Birgitta 108
Vivaldi, Antonio 72
Värnlund, Rudolf 30

Wahlöö, Per 128
Wajda, Andrzej 73
Waldekranz, Rune 5, 47, 68
Weiss, Peter 59
Wenders, Wim 124
Wiberg, Franz G. 6
Widerberg, Bo 24, 64, 65, 67, 68, **69—73**, 80, 81, 96, 98, **99**, 108, 112, 128, 129, 146
Wigforss, Ernst 28
Wikholm, Claire 100
Wilde, Oscar 50
Wollter, Sven 129
Wållgren, Gun 142
Wästberg, Per 126

Yeats, W. B. 99

Zetterberg, Hanna 146
Zetterling, Mai 36, 38, 39, 68, 70, **77—79**, 146

Åberg, Lasse 115
Åhlin, Per 130

ACKNOWLEDGEMENTS
The author would like to extend his thanks to the following for their help and support during the production of this book: Olle Rosberg at the Swedish Film Institute, Ove Svensson and Jennifer Sundberg at the Swedish Institute and Kjell Albin Abrahamson.

Photographs by courtesy of the Swedish Film Institute, AB Svensk Filmindustri, Cinematograph AB, Europa Film, Sandrew Film och Teater AB.
Cover photos: top *Ingeborg Holm* (The Swedish Film Institute), centre *Miss Julie* (Sandrew Film och Teater AB), front *Fanny and Alexander* (Cinematograph AB).